Dan Perjovschi
THE PRIZE BOOK

Hamburger Kunsthalle
Koenig Books, London

THE PRIZE BOOK

2016

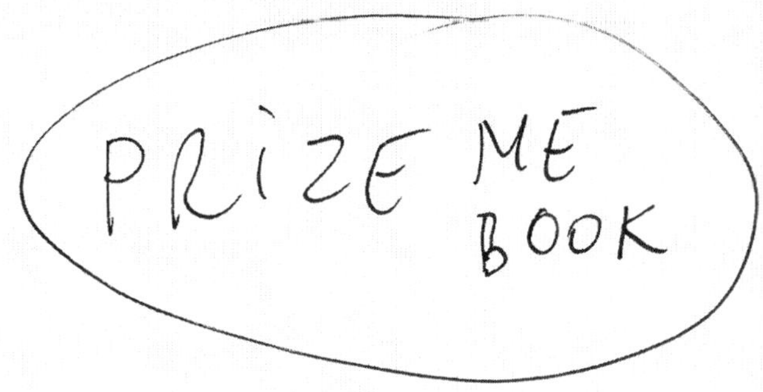

HAMBURG

OCT 2016

A — SOME THOUGHTS BEFORE

B — GOING TO...

C — IN THE ACTION

D — POST FACTUM

THE PRICE
OF PRIZE

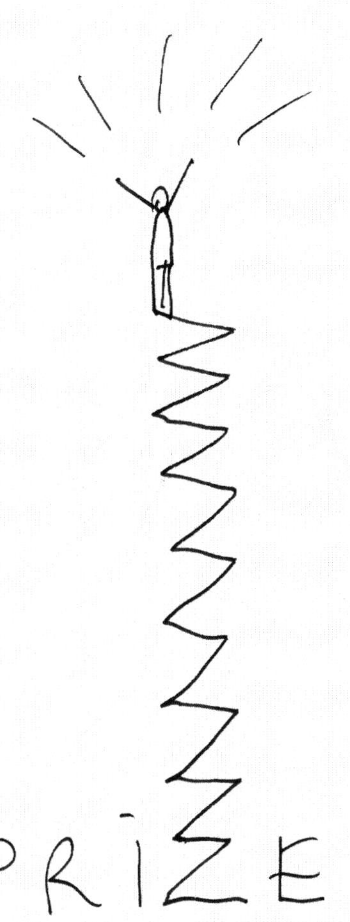
PRIZE

GOT
ROJA!

who's rosa?

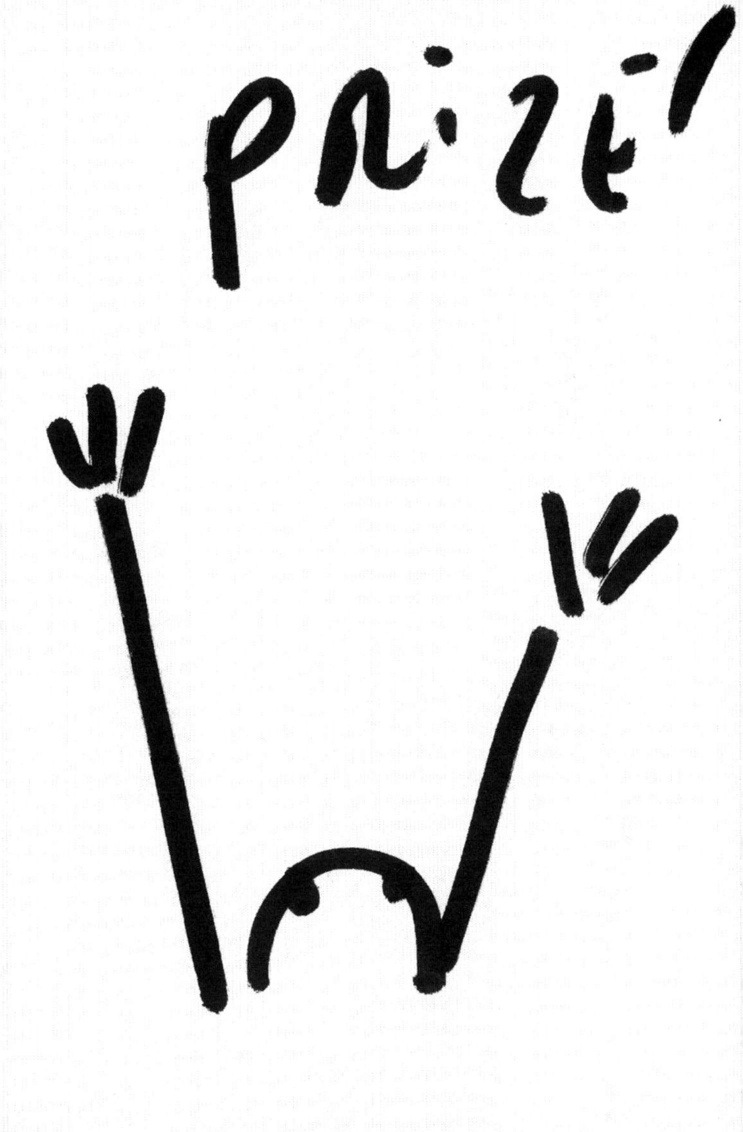

prize

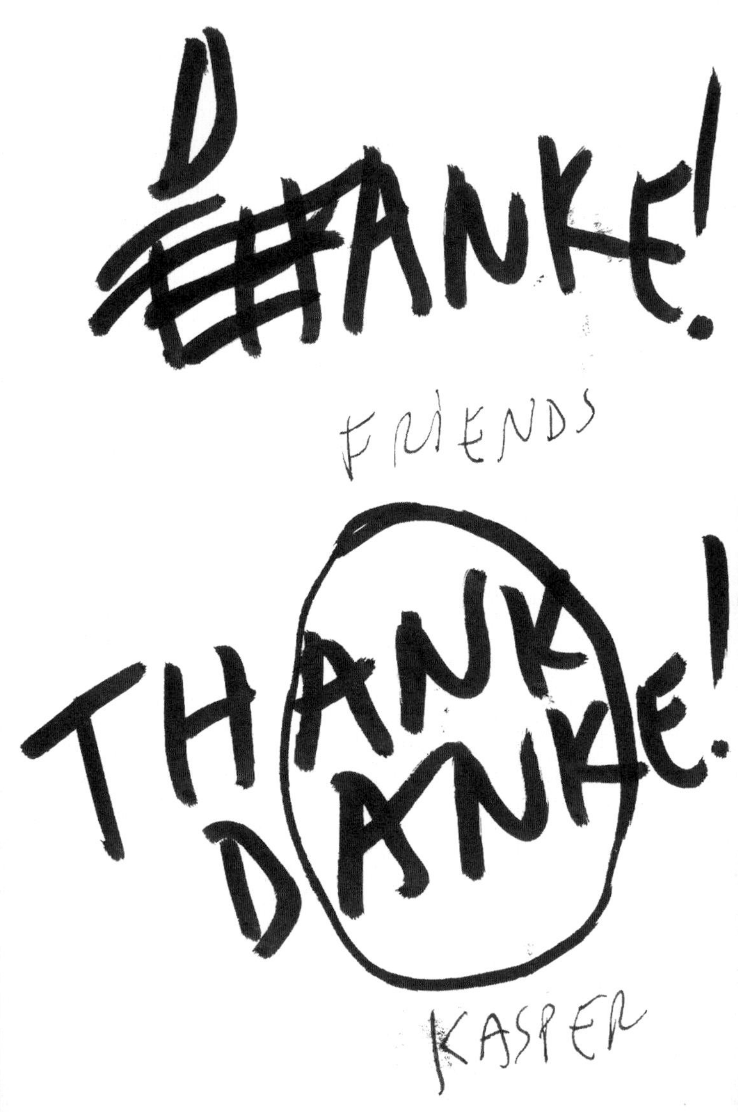

DEFANKE!
FRIENDS
THANK
DANKE!
KASPER

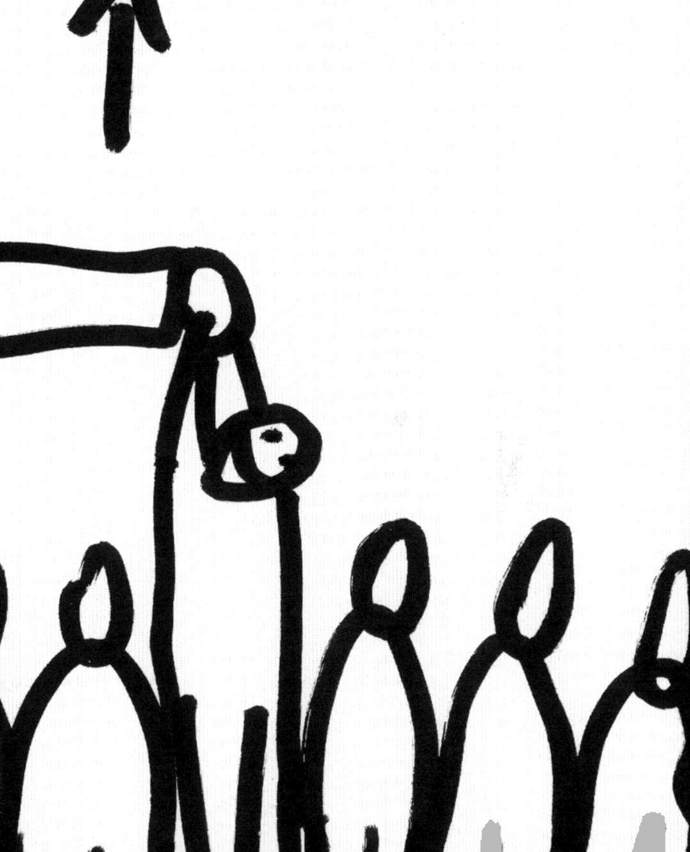
PRIZE

DAN KE!

Perjovschi

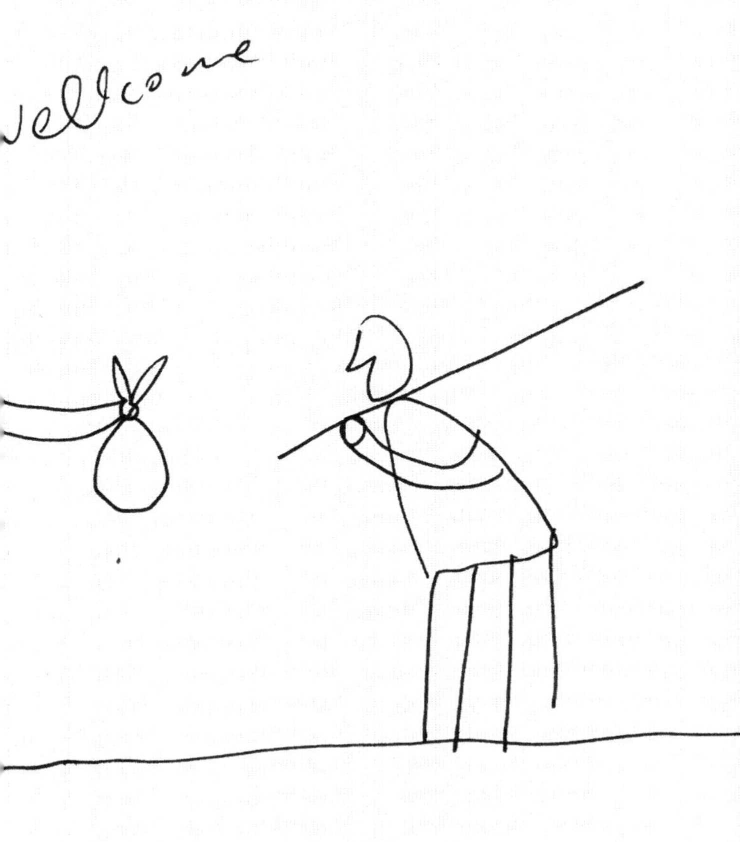

Welcome

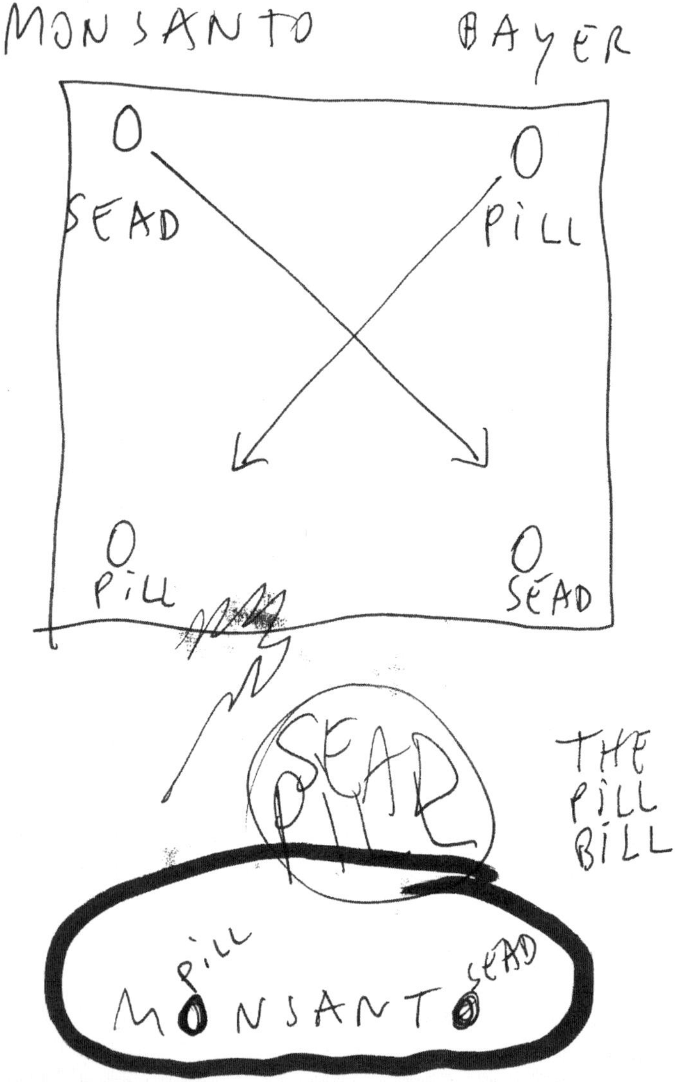

MONSANTO
BAYER
O SEAD
O PILL
O PILL
O SEAD
SEAD
PILL
THE PILL BILL
PILL
MONSANTO
SEAD

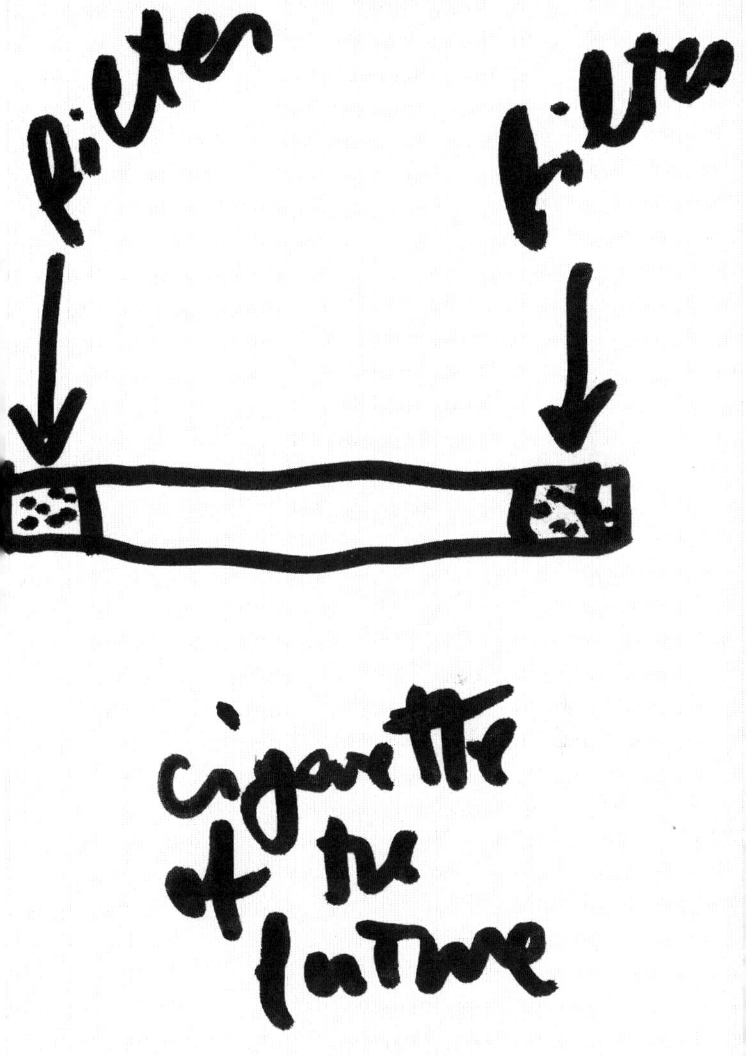

filter
filter
cigarette
of the
future

MANTERRUPTING

MANSPLAINING

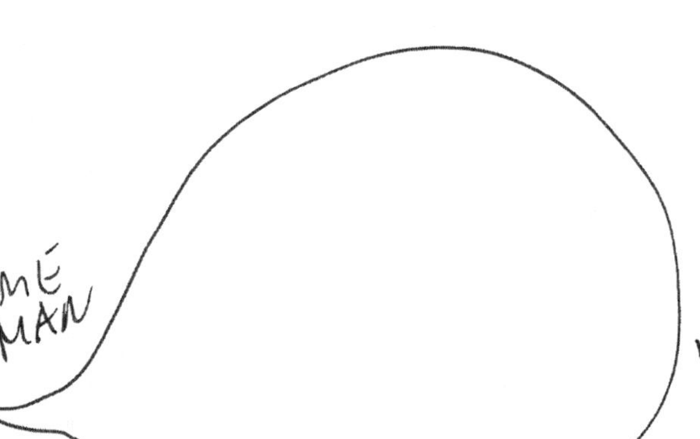

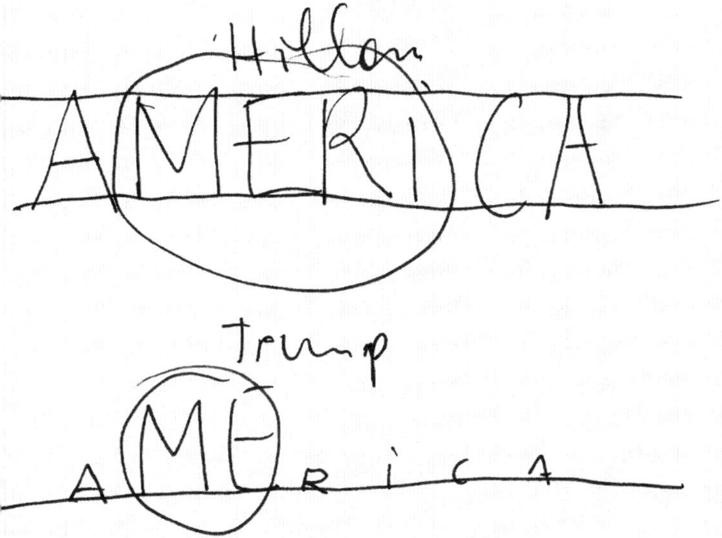

Hillary
AMERICA
Trump
AMERICA

MAKE
ME
AMERICA
GREAT
AGAIN
TRUMP

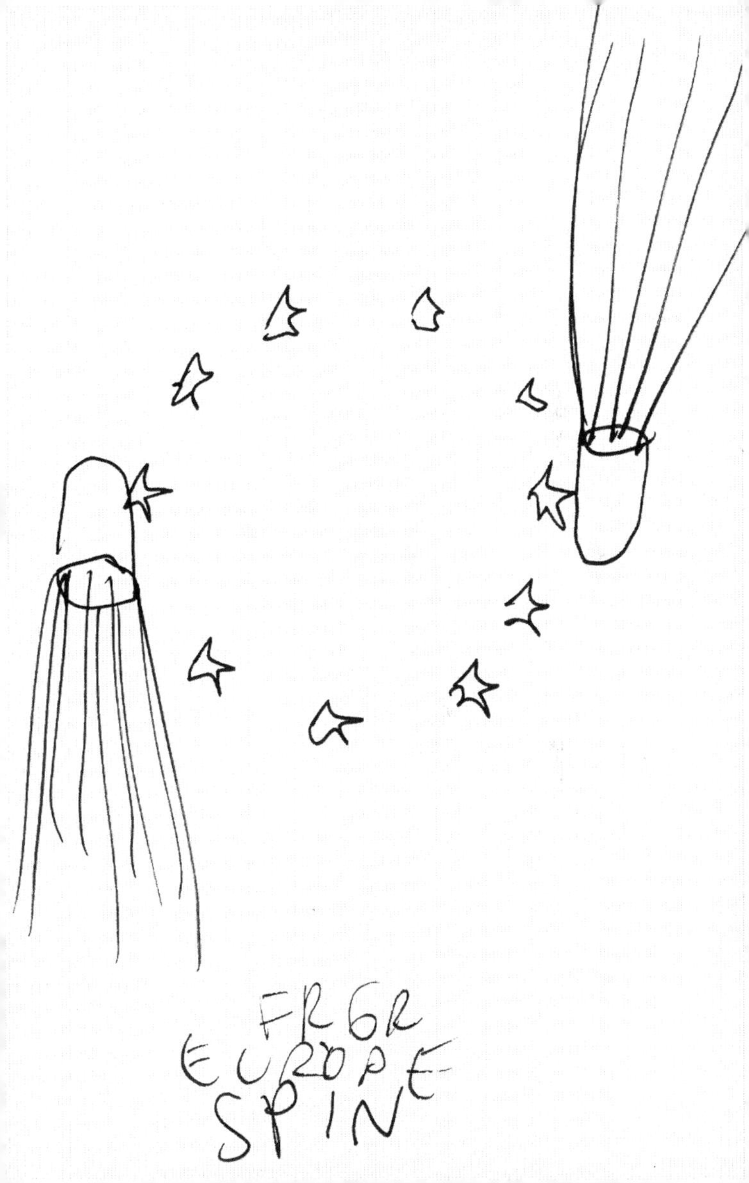

FR GR
EUROPE
SPIN

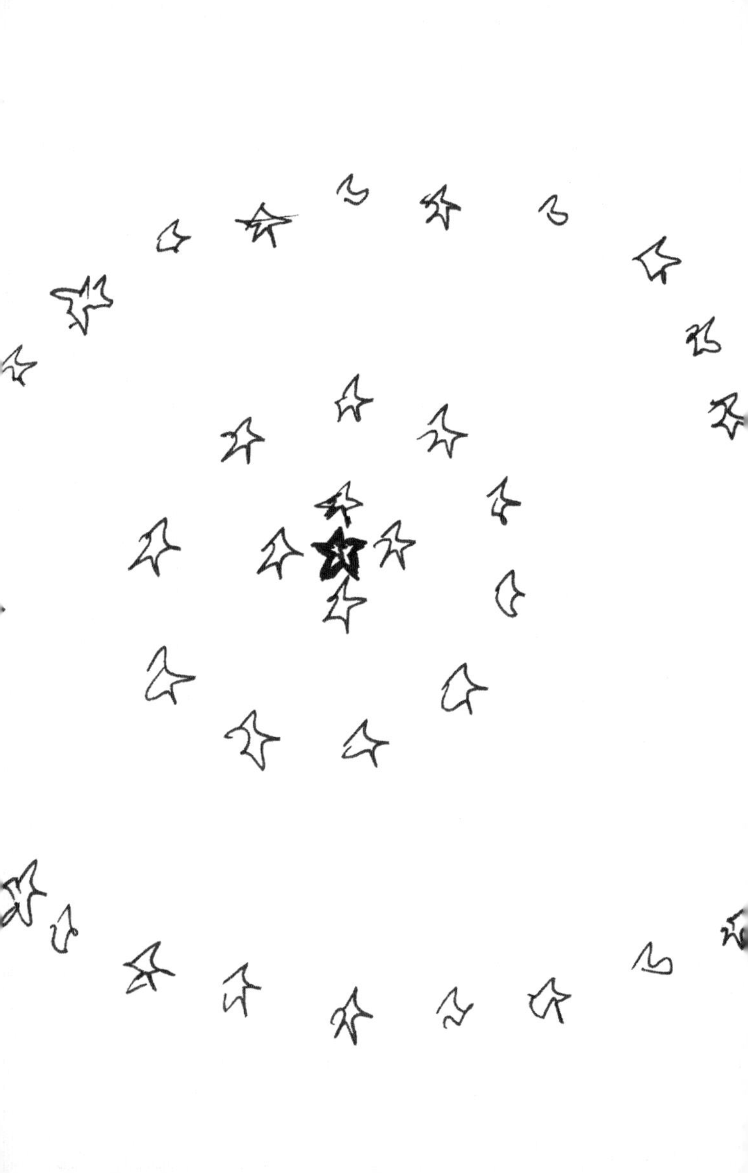

TURKEY
UK

INSTEAD

TAKE
TURKEY INSTEAD

BORIS TALK

DANGERS

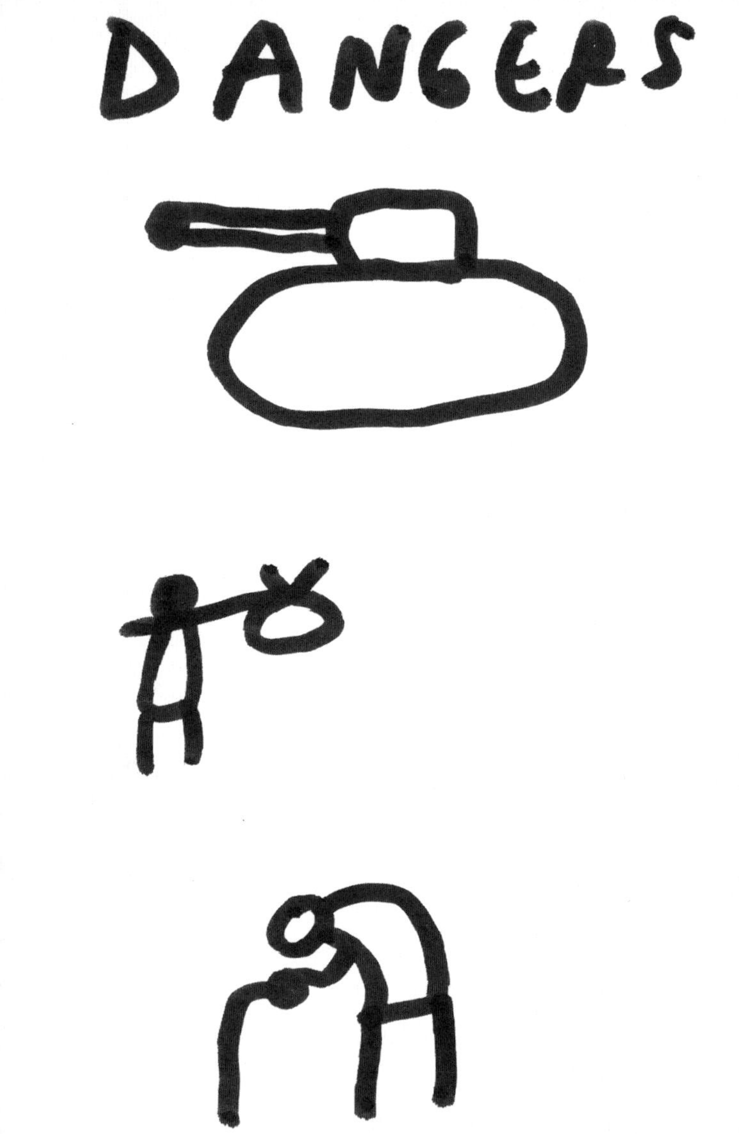

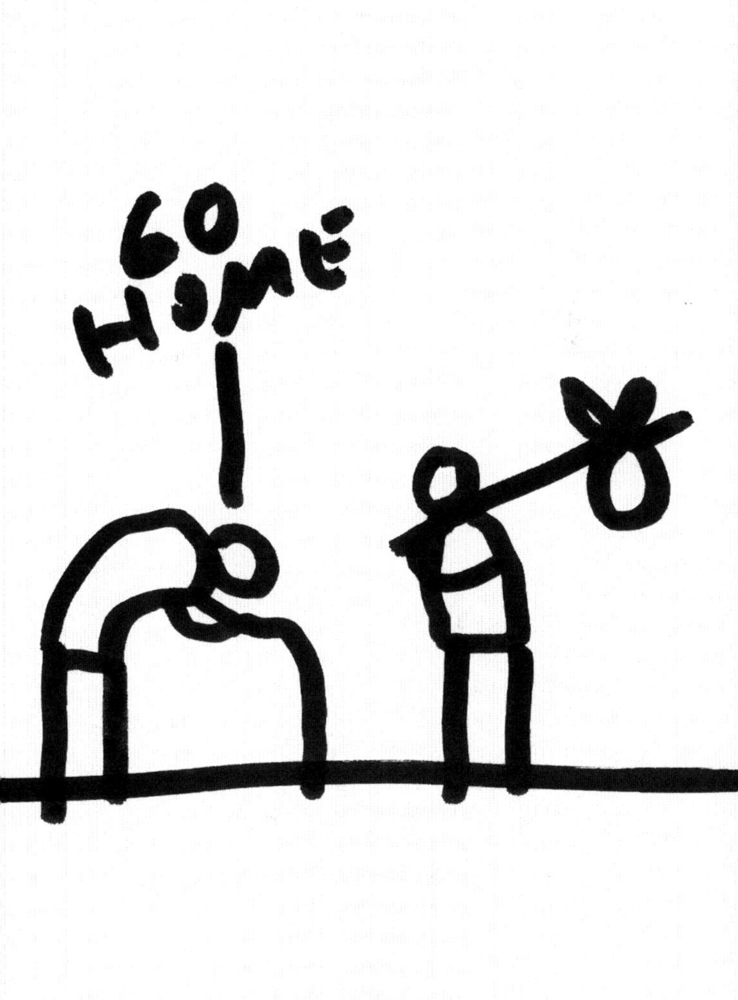

GO
HOME

BIRD VIEW

EYE LEVEL

SHÉISE!

PARDON
MY
FRENCH

NOT
AGAIN...

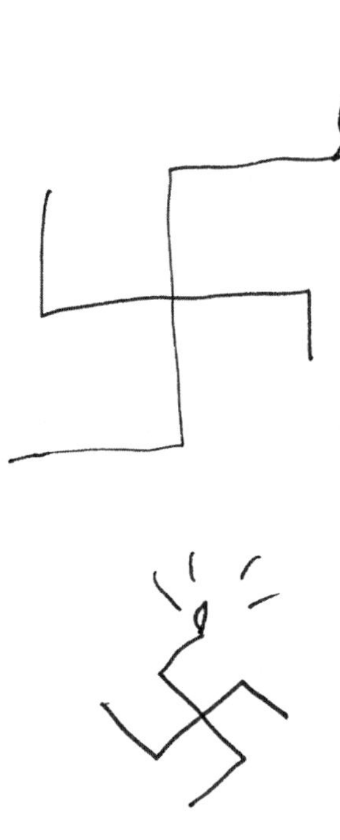

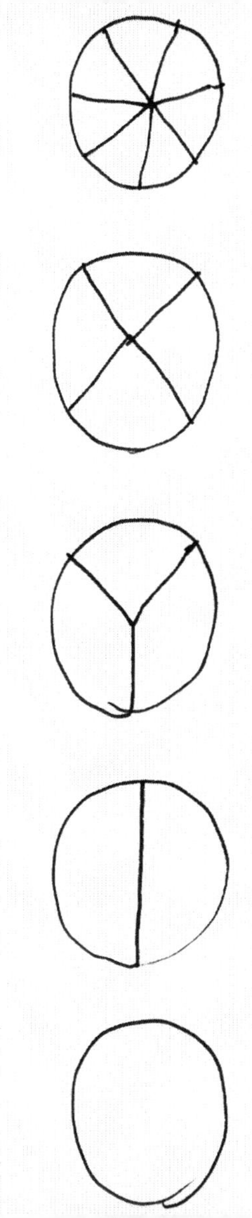

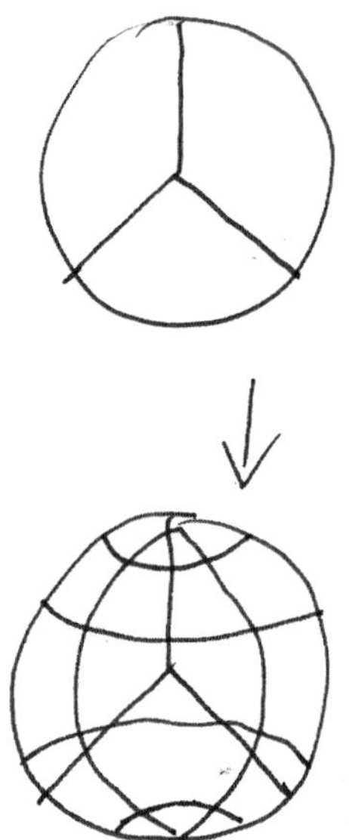

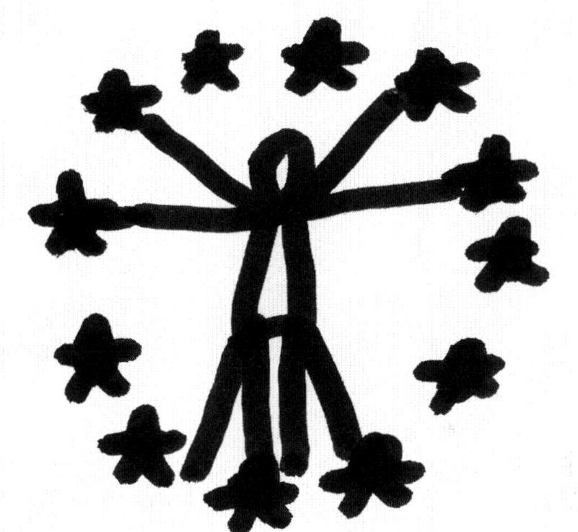

OLD
NEW

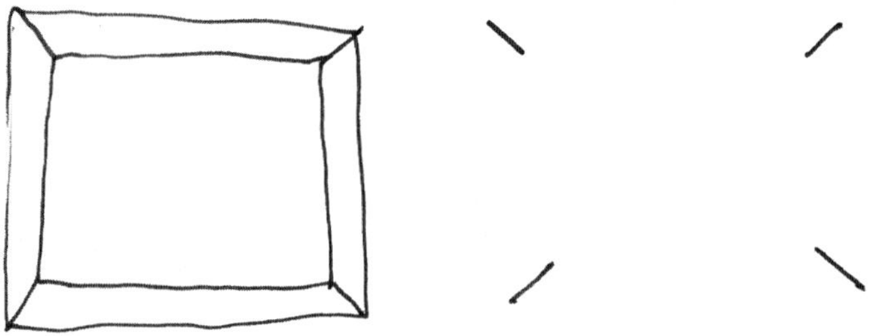

ART

ART IN
COLLECTION

KUNSTHALLE NEU

KUNST HALLÉ

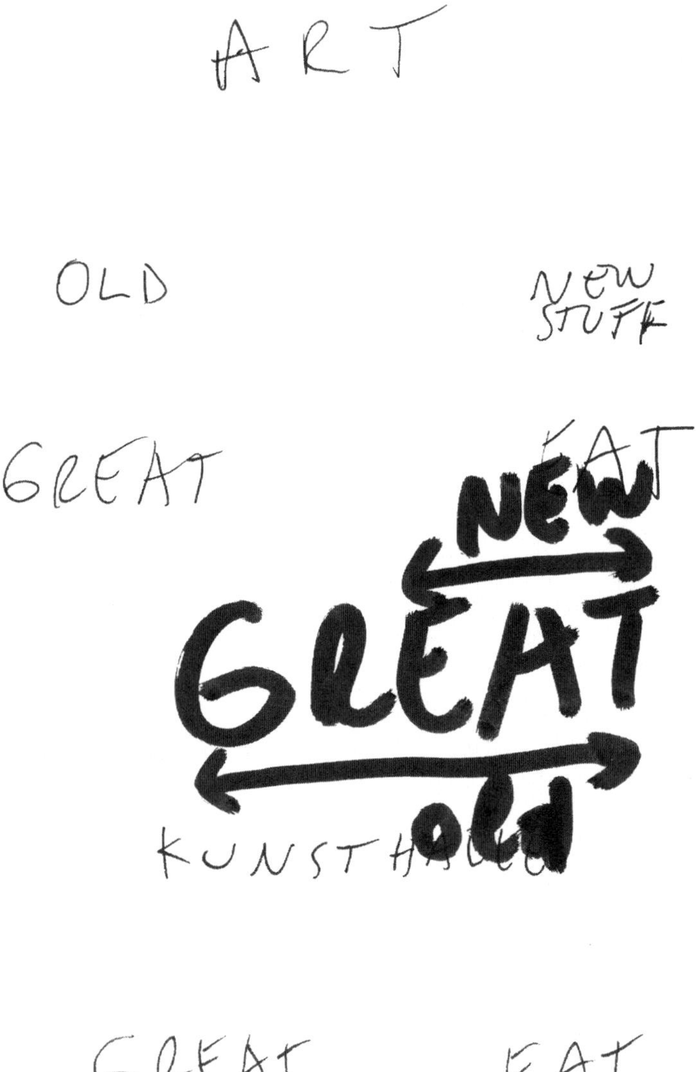

ART
OLD
NEW
STUFF
GREAT
NEAT
EAT
NEW
GREAT
OLD
KUNSTHALLE
GREAT
EAT

DEUTSCHE

BANG

BANG

OH NO
NOT DEUTSCHE
BANK!!

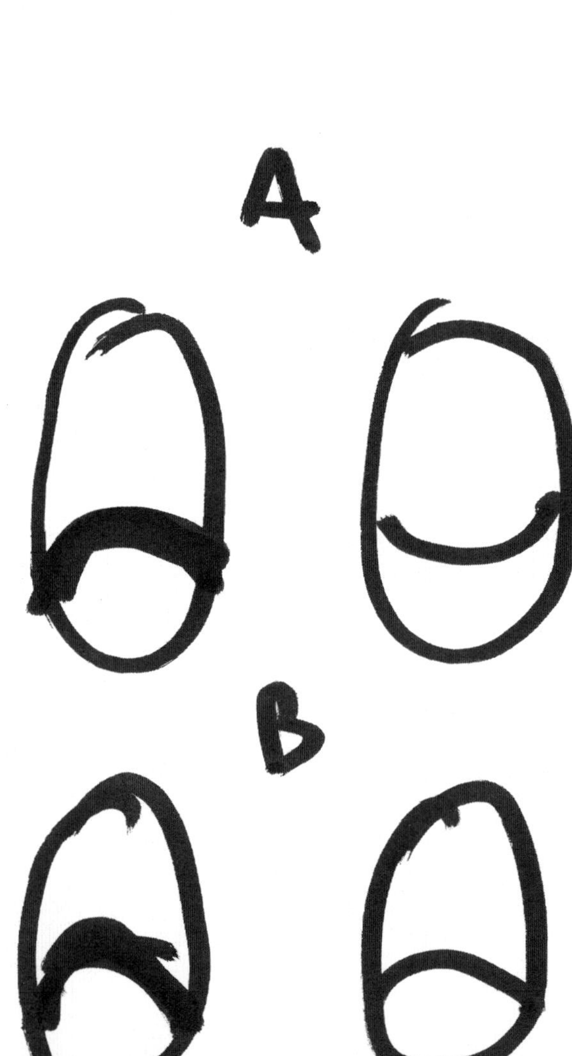

A
B

THE ~~HUMAN~~ RIGHT

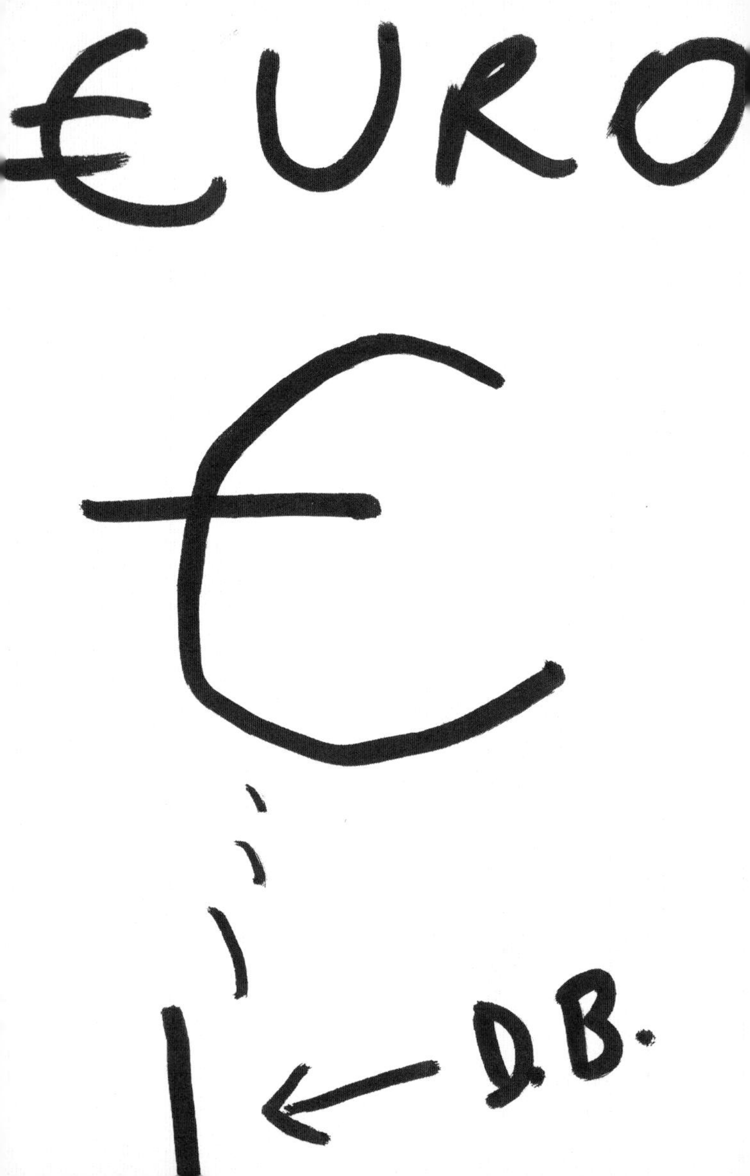

EURO
€
€ ← DB.

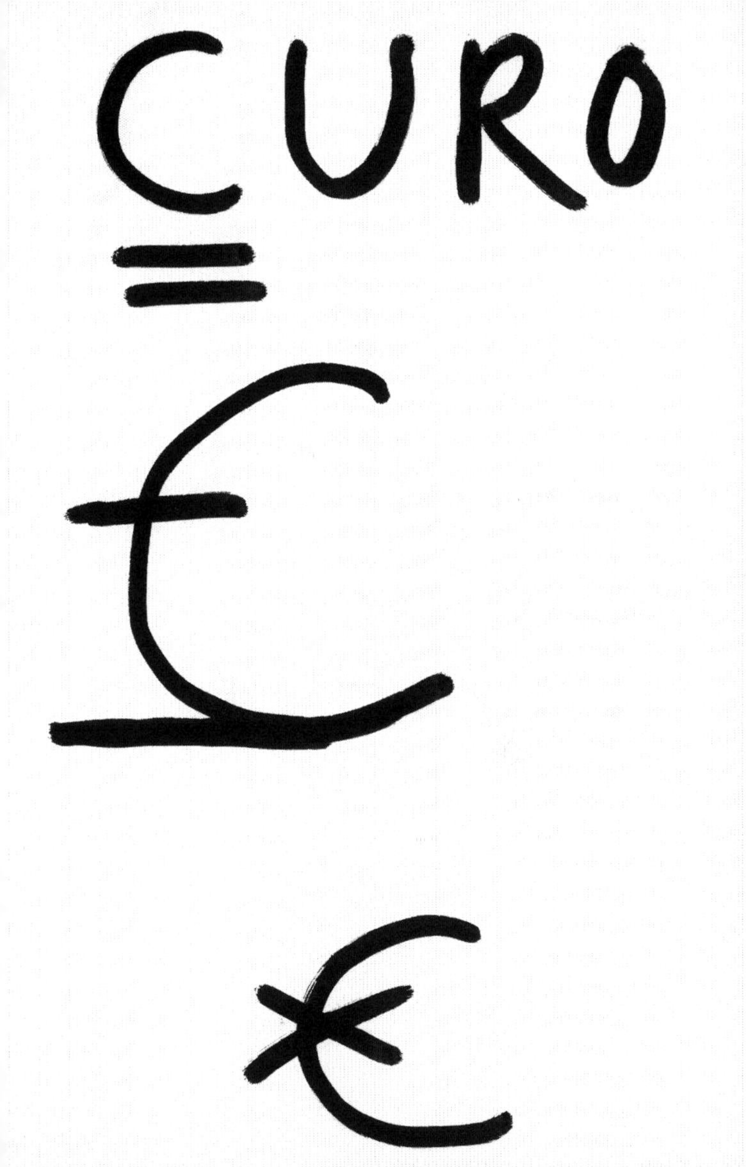

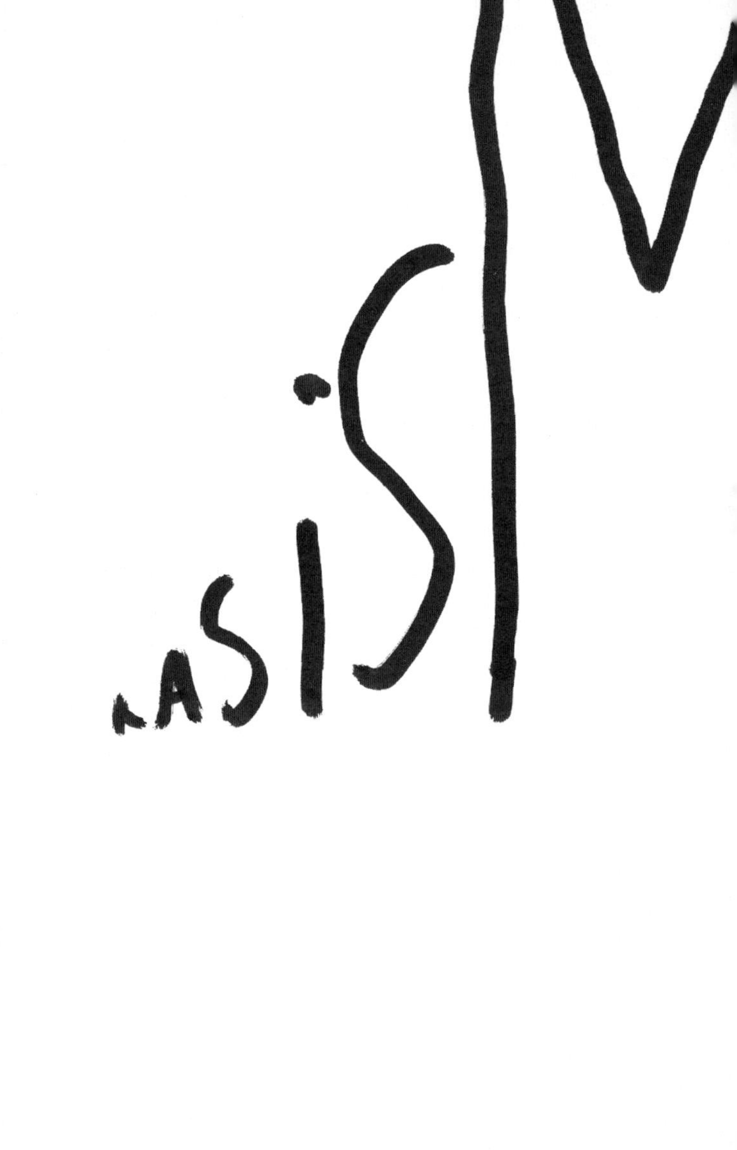

EXTREME HUMAN RIGHT

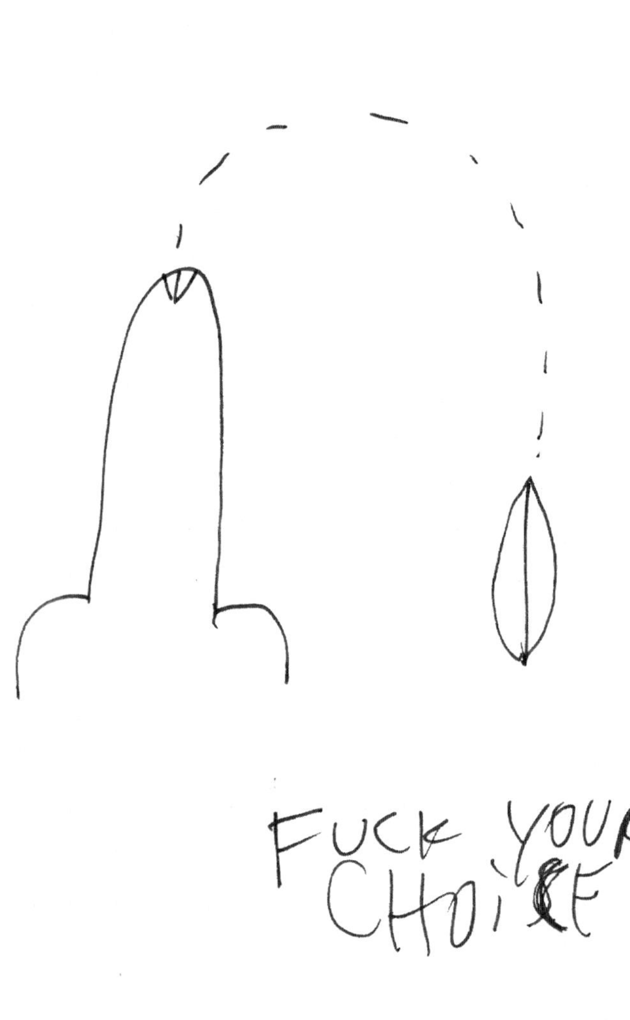

FUCK YOUR CHOICE
POLAND AND.....

UTERUS
POLAND

POLAND
BATTLEFIELD

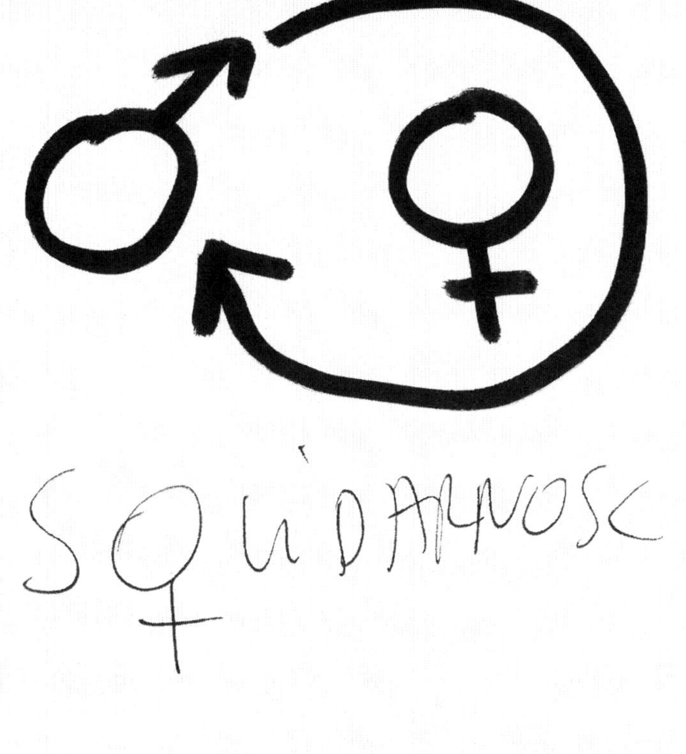

SOLIDARNOSC
POLAND

SIXTY?!!!!!

I DID 60 SHOWS
IN GERMANY
BUT THIS COUNTRY
HAS 300
KUNSTVEREINS &
KUNSTHALLES
SO I HAVE
LOTS MORE
STUFF TO DO

LIST OF KUNSTHALLE KUNSTVEREIN
& MUSEUMS

GÖPINGEN
LUBECK
LINGEN
PORTIKUS
HAMBURG KUNSTVEREIN
HARTWARE KUNSTVEREIN
WURTEMBERGISCHE KUNSTVEREIN
KIEL
ULM

HALE --- LEIPZIG
SINGEN MUSEUM
LUDWIG MUSEUM KÖLN
INTERNATIONAL FORUM AACHEN
LENBACHAUS
MARTA
MUSEUM OF MODERN ART FRANKFULT

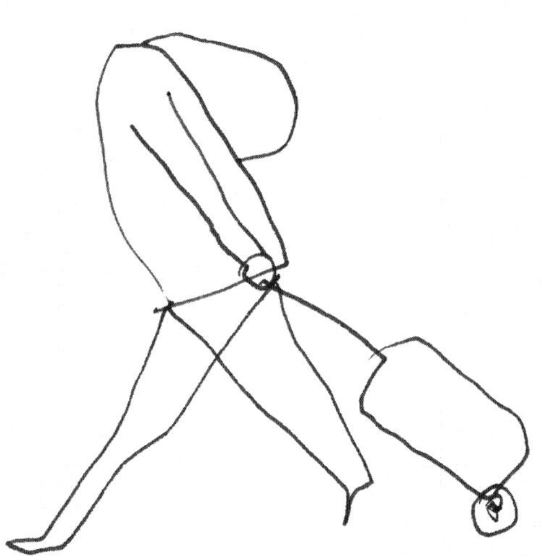

WHAT DO Y ?
FORGOT ?

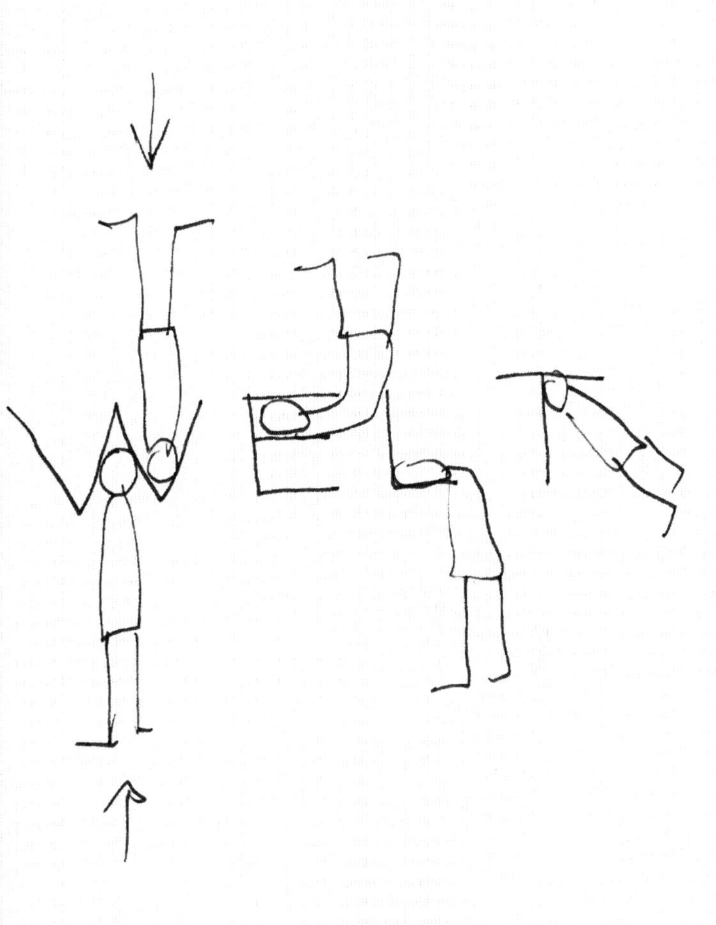

IELT

WELT

WELT

ELT

WELT WELT
→
WELT → WELT

ENTRANCE ME
TO
MASTERS   THEM

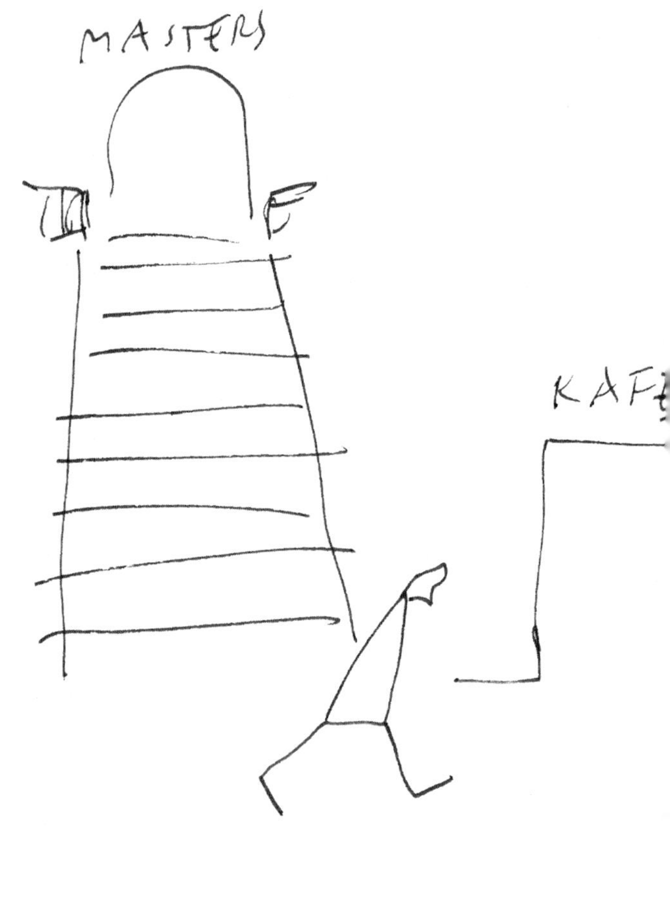
MASTERS
KAFE
PRO CHOICE

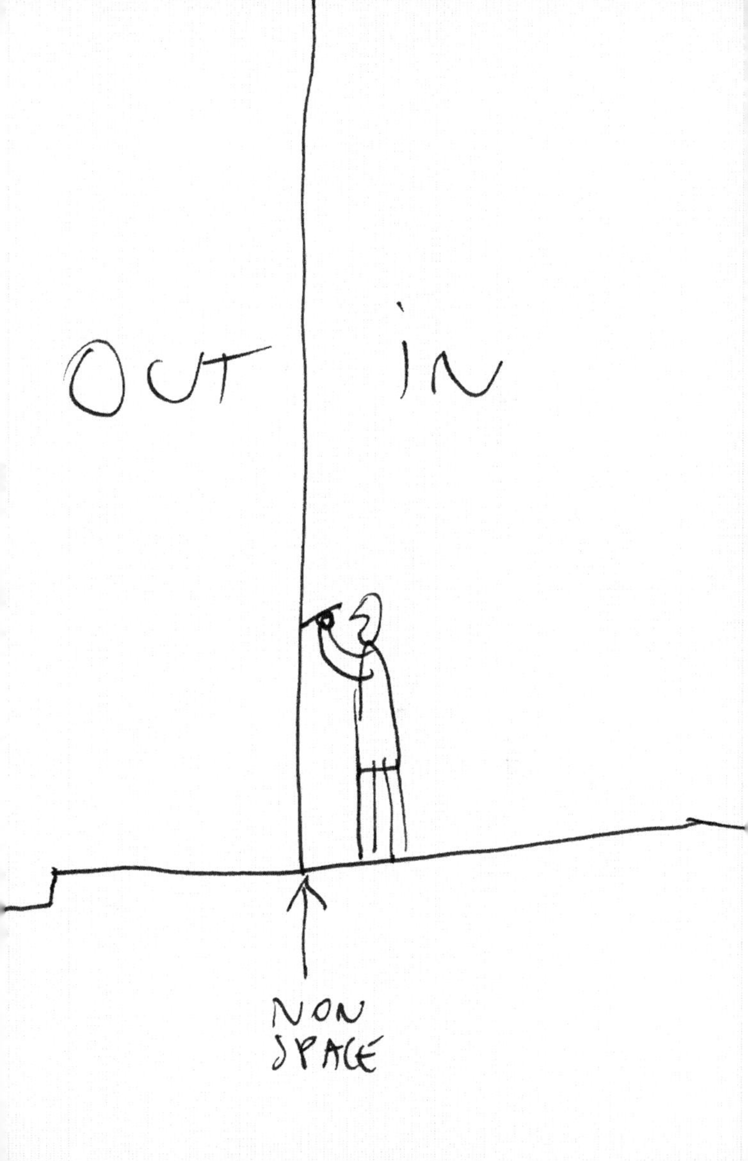

OUT
IN
NON
SPACE

ALT   NEUE
OLD   NEW
KUNSTHALLE

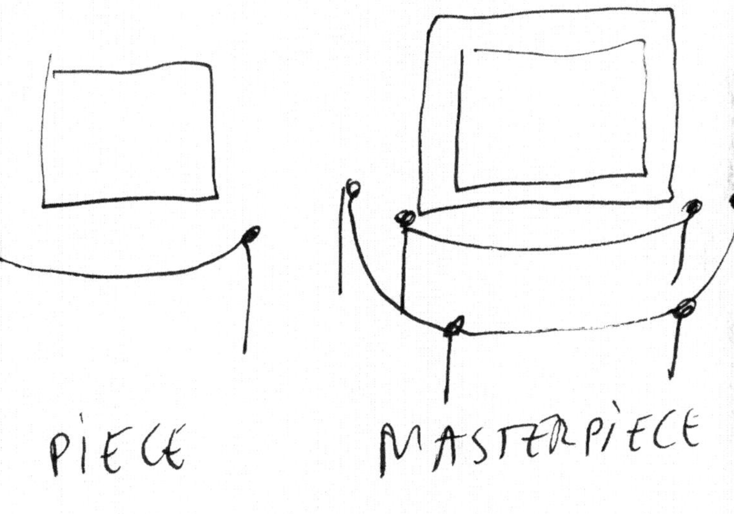

PIECE
MASTERPIECE

KUNSTMUSEUM
KUNSTHALLE,
KUNSTVEREIN
KUNSTHAUS
KUNSTKUNST

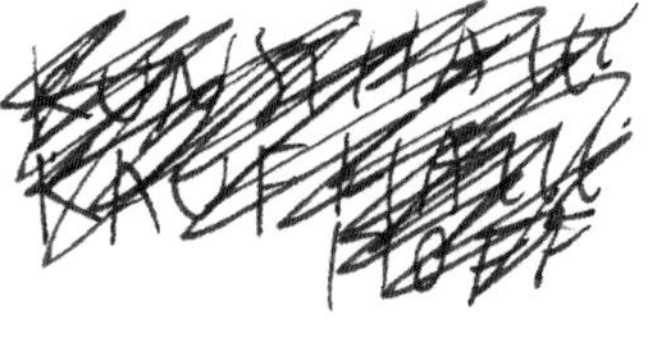

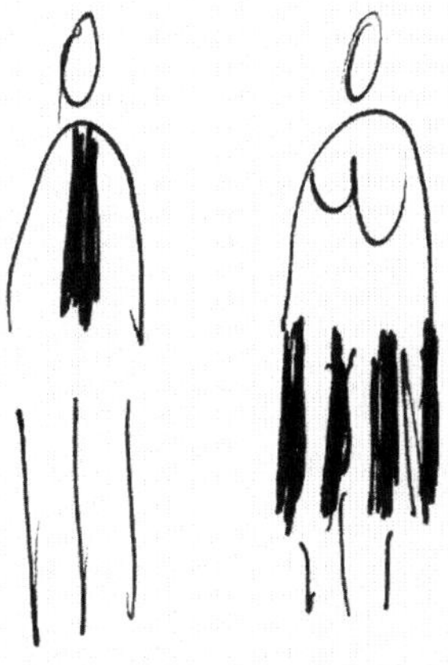

MAN WORLD

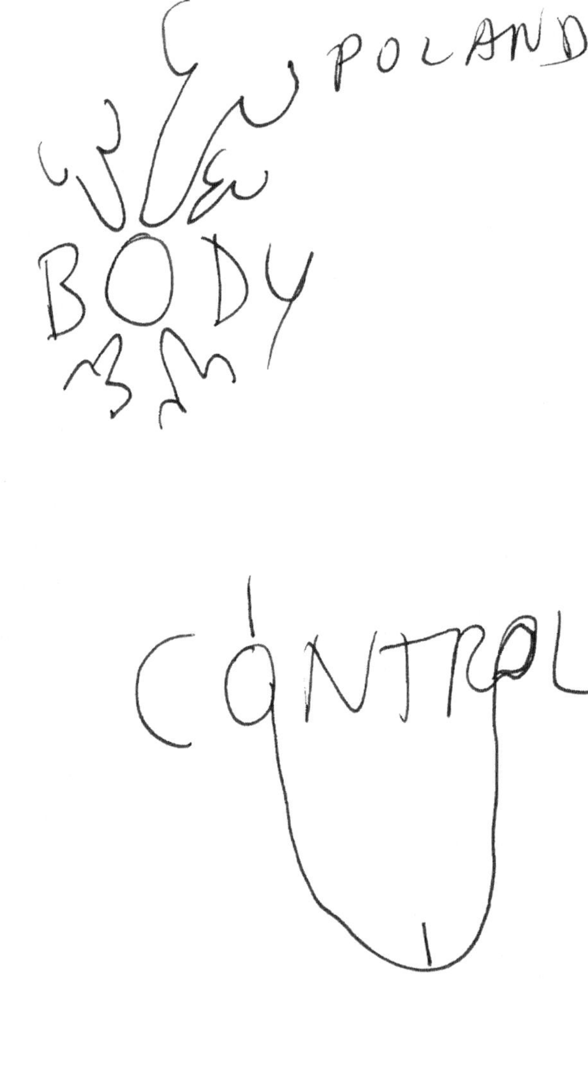
NEW
POLAND
BODY
CONTROL

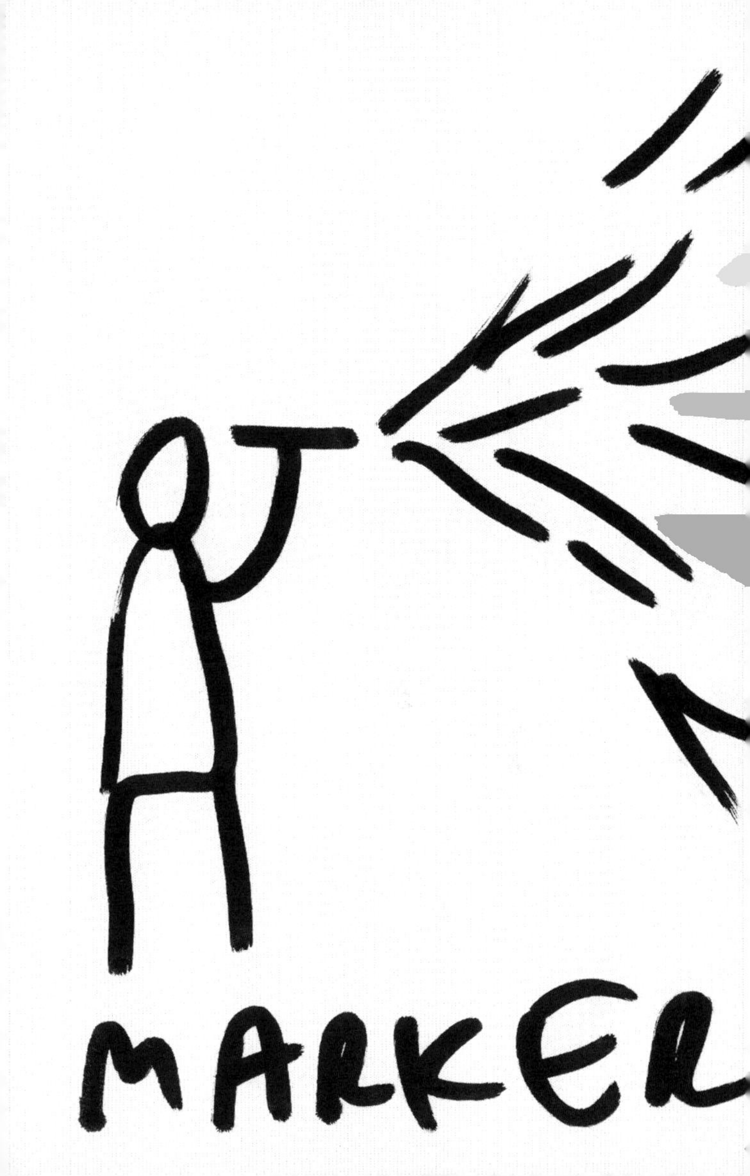

MARKER

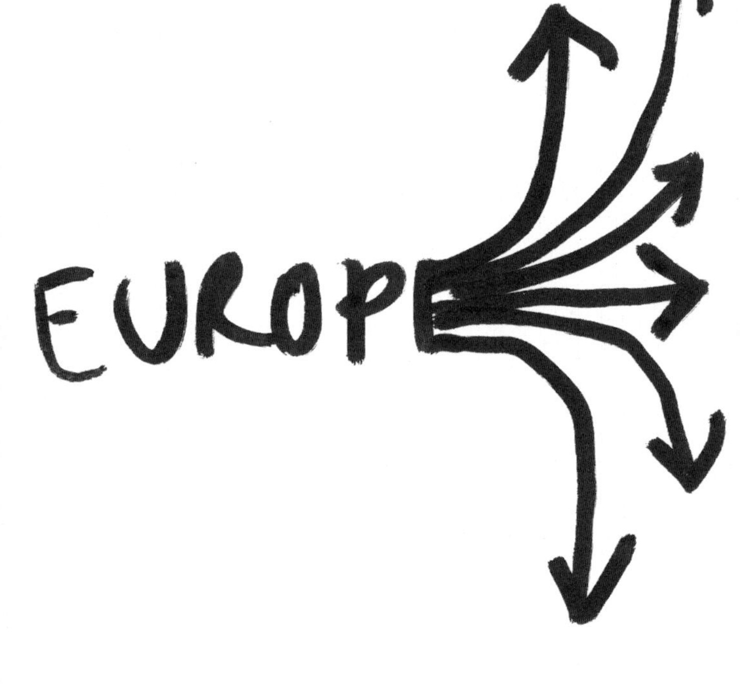

EUROPE

CORE COUNTRIES AND EDGE COUNTRIES

europa

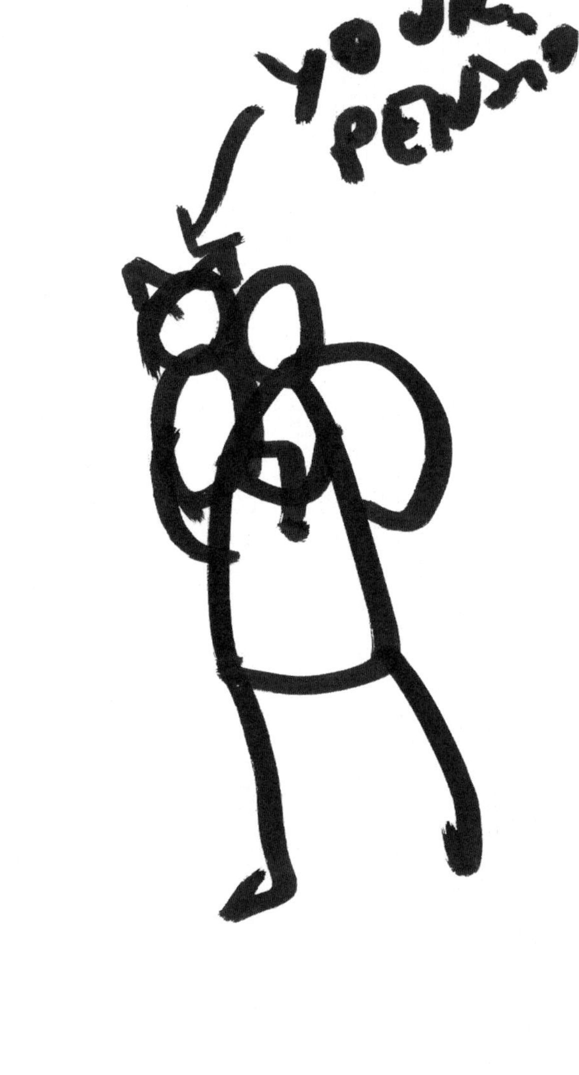
YOUR
PENSION

1189
___

HUNGARY

| | | | |

2016

THE NIGHT
HURRICANE

THE WIND
FROM THE
RIGHT

THE OTHER

O   R

THE   THE

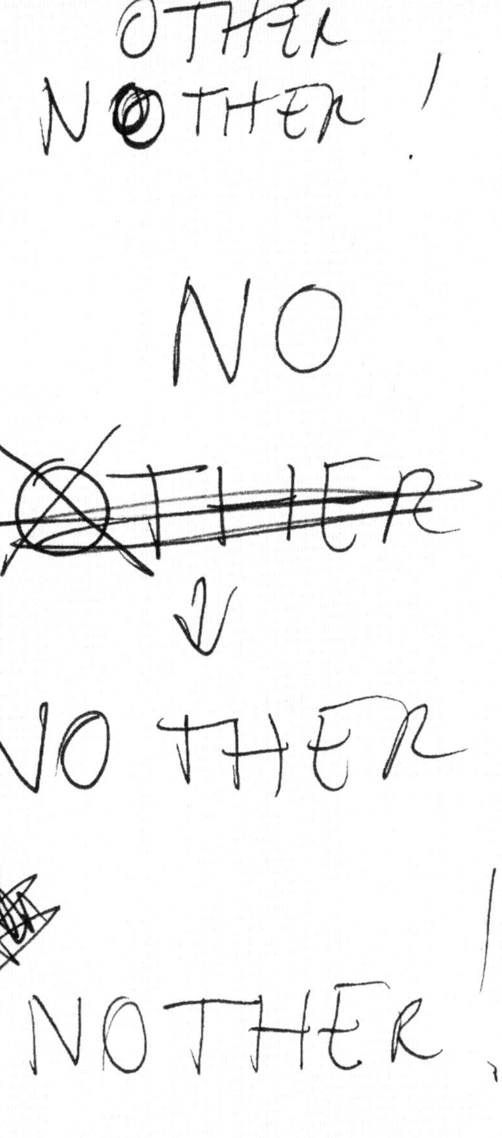

OTHER
NOTHER!
NO
OTHER
NO THER
NOTHER!

RA US TONOMY

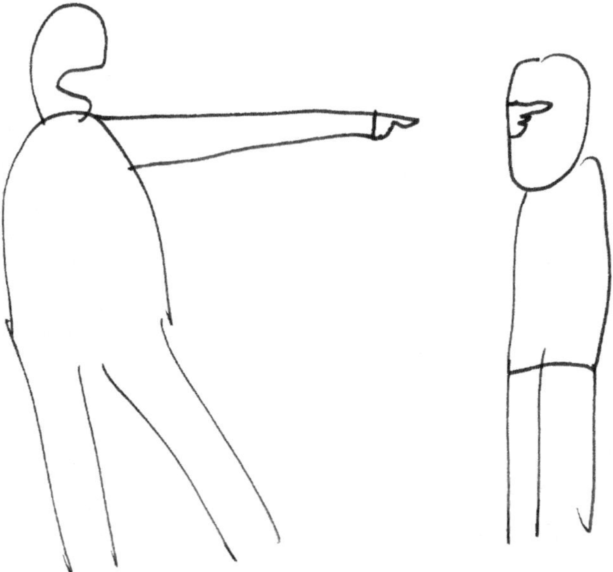

HAMBURG
P ORT

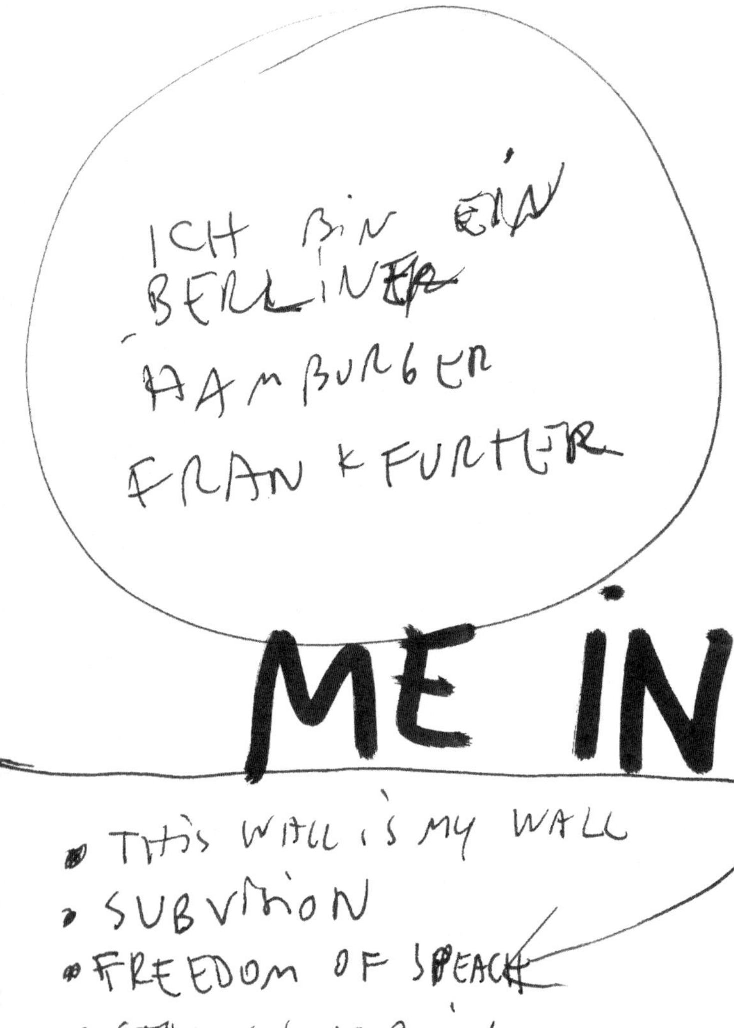

ICH BIN EIN
BERLINER
HAMBURGER
FRANKFURTER
ME IN
THIS WALL IS MY WALL
SUBVIION
FREEDOM OF SPEACH
STADKURATORIN
ROSA XHAPIRE

AME ♡ HAMBURG:
A LONG STORY.
FIRST THIS WALL WAS MINE
HAN] WAS IN A
CONTAINER AND
FREE OF SPEECH
AND INSERTED IN THE
LOCAL
NEWSPAPERS
AND NOW
I GOT ROSA
HAMBURL

KUNST

KUNST

KUNST ← prize

NOBEL TO COLOMBIA
CLIMATE?

THE WAY YOU
DRESS

THE WAY YOU
BORN

WATCH YOUR LANGUAGE
MAD   AN
GENTLE   MAN

MAD AN

VIRTUAL
REALITY
IS
THE
REALITY

YES   NO   I DON'T
              KNOW

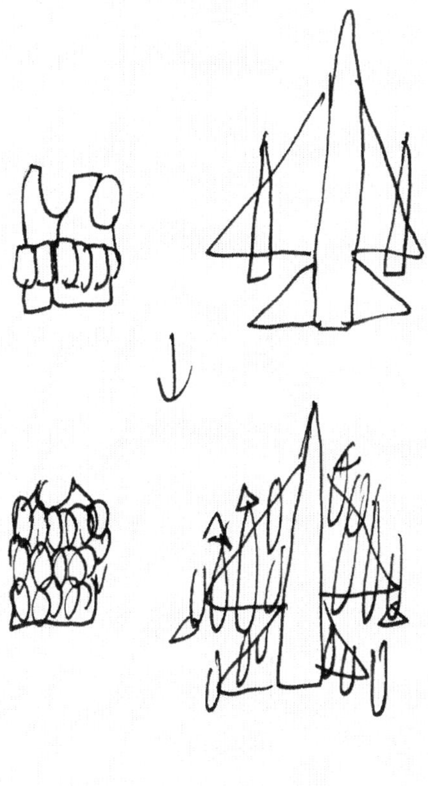

ASYMETRIC
WAR

MAIN STREAM

MANY STREAM

ALTERNATIVE

STREAM OUT THE MAIN

europa

then   vs

MEN ARE
DIRECTORS

WOMEN ARE.
CURATORS

GOT FRIENDS

WELLCOME

WELL ...

KALTE
KRIEG
KRISE

KKK

COLD WAR IN TIMES OF GLOBAL WARMING

COLOMBIA

SÍ

NO

NOBEL

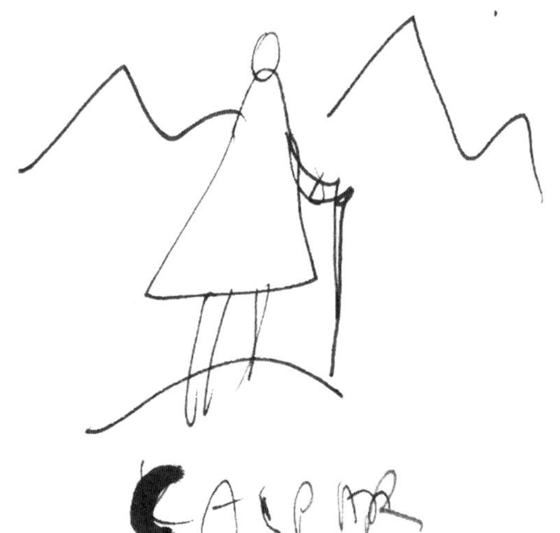

CASPAR

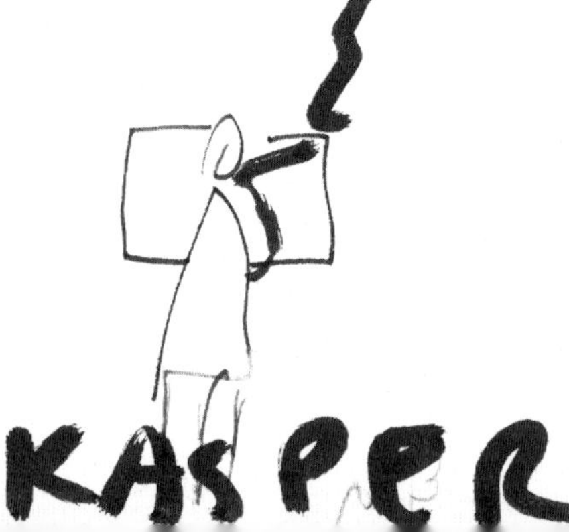

KASPER

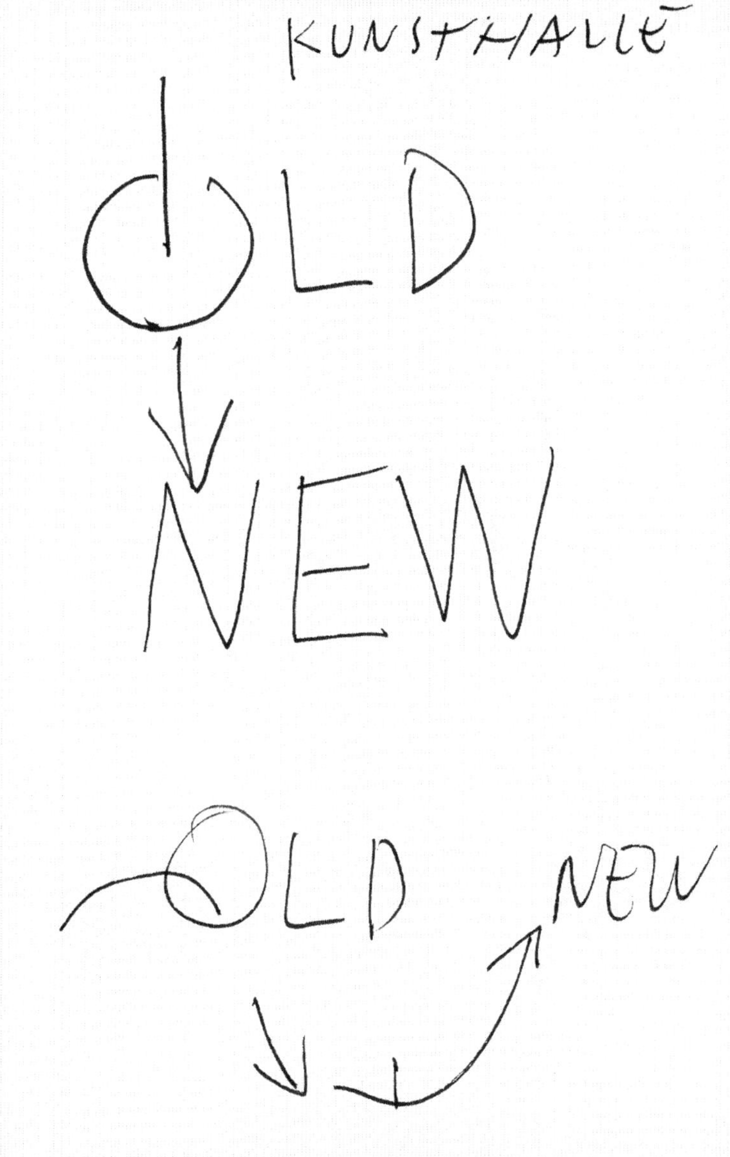

KUNSTHALLE
OLD
NEW
OLD
NEW

HUNGARY

1985

2016

in 1985 They open the
borders for east germens
in 2016 they erect
walls . .

TRUMP is
A PUSSY

TRUMPUSSY

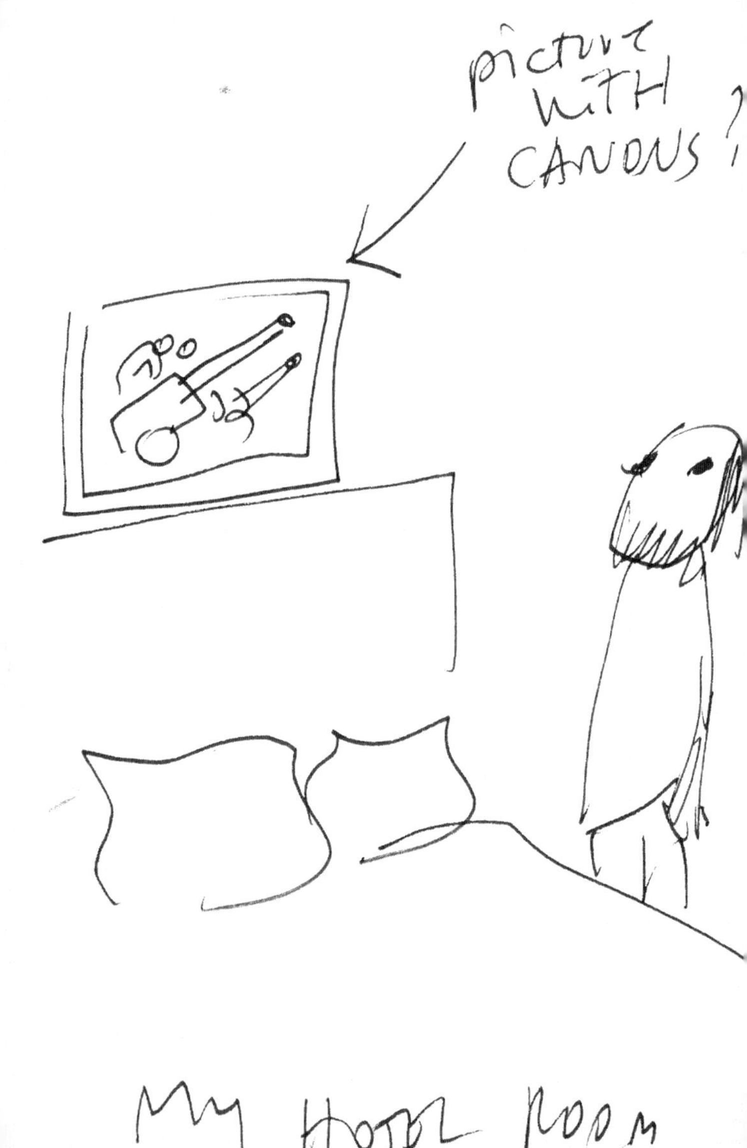

picture WITH CANONS?
MY HOTEL ROOM

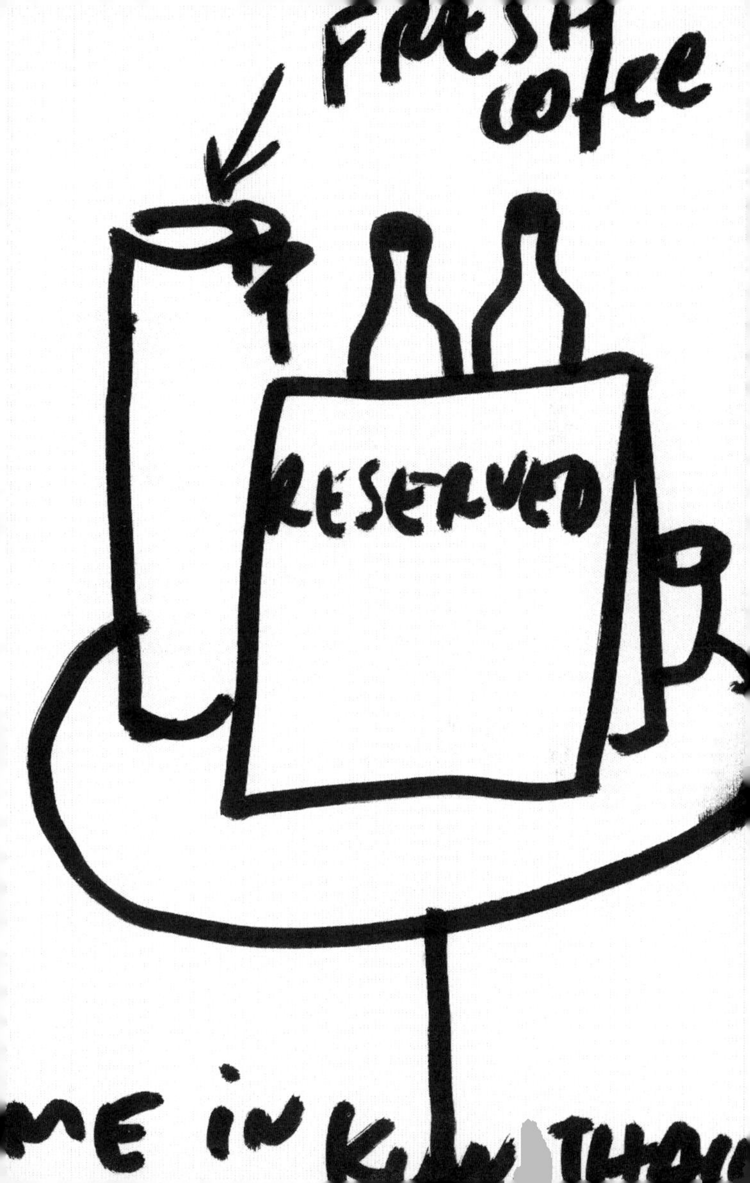

FRESH
cofee
RESERVED
ME iN K...

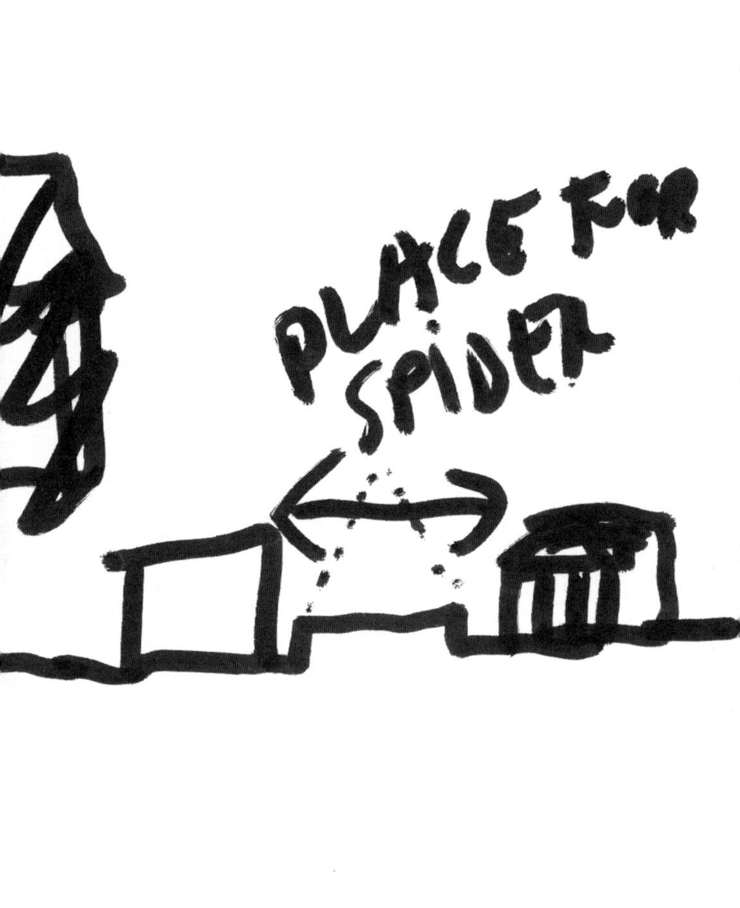
PLACE FOR
SPIDER

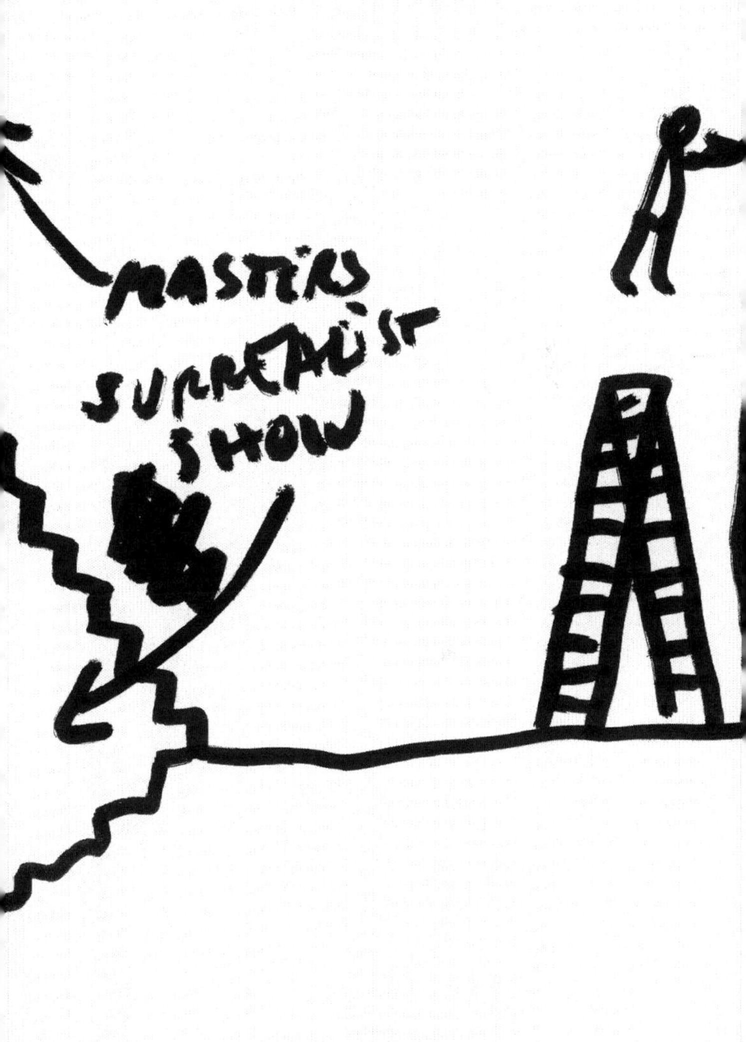

MASTERS
SURREALIST
SHOW

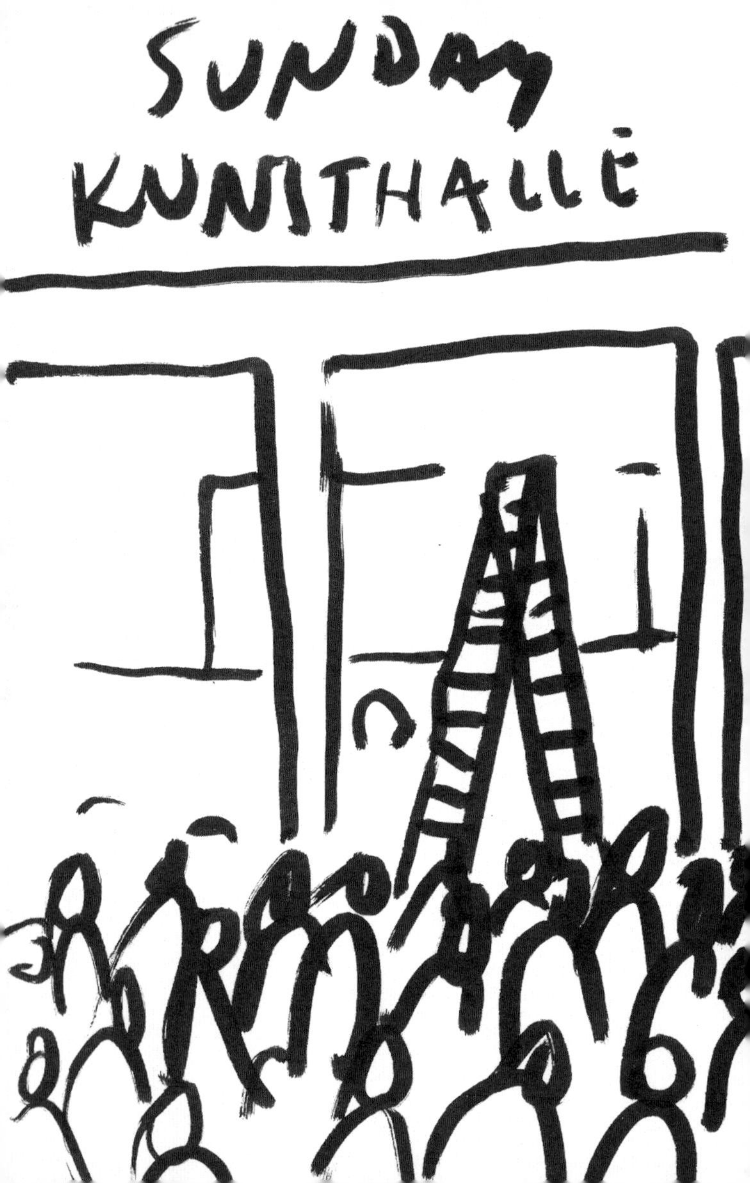

SUNDAY
KUNSTHALLE

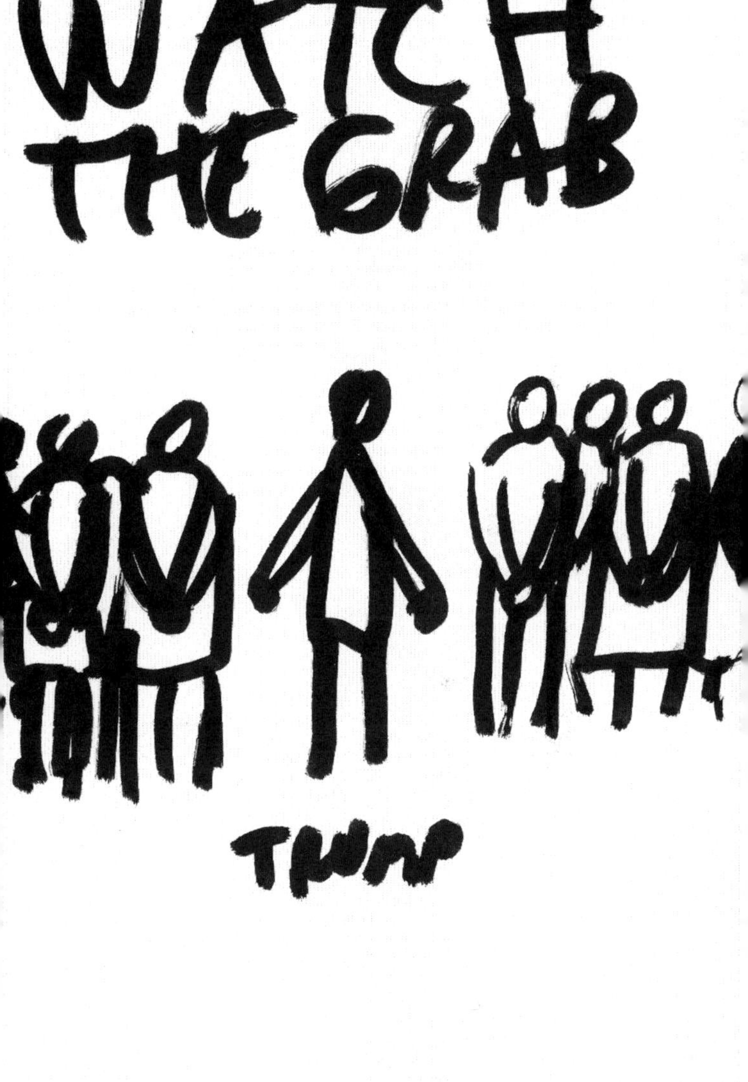

WATCH
THE GRAB
TRUMP

WHEN KID
I COULD NOT
TOUCH NO WALL.

NOW

THEY

PAY ME

TO...

F-22
F-15
~~GOD~~
HELP
US

CLINTON/OBAMA

ABU GHRAIB

TRUMP

GRAB

BAD
NEOLIBERAL

WORSE
NONLIBERAL

PARADISE:

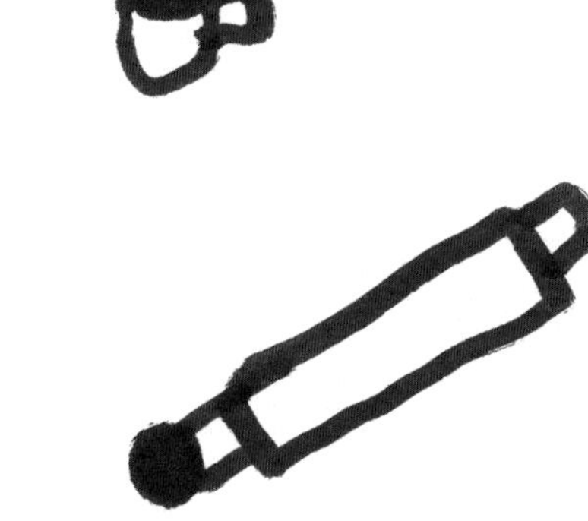

BOMB ON

chemnitz

LIE DOWN

LIES UP

HATE
ATE
US

WAJDA
GONE

GER MANY

GERMAN EXPORT
RECORD: BIGGEST
EVER

GERMAN IMPORT
RECORD: ME

96.5 billion euro

20.000 + 10.000
Peasy Peasy

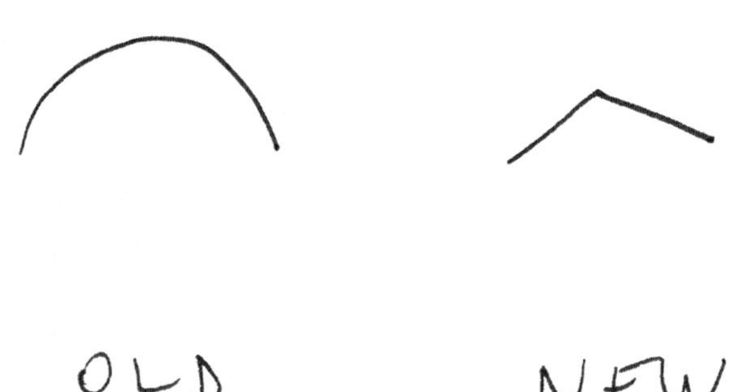

KUNSTHALLE

OLD   NEW

ICHELANGELO   A GUY
   DA VINCI   FROM
                      MEXICO

        OLD | NEW

  DA VINCI | A GUY FRo-
    DALI | MEXICO
               | -ME
          DA | DA

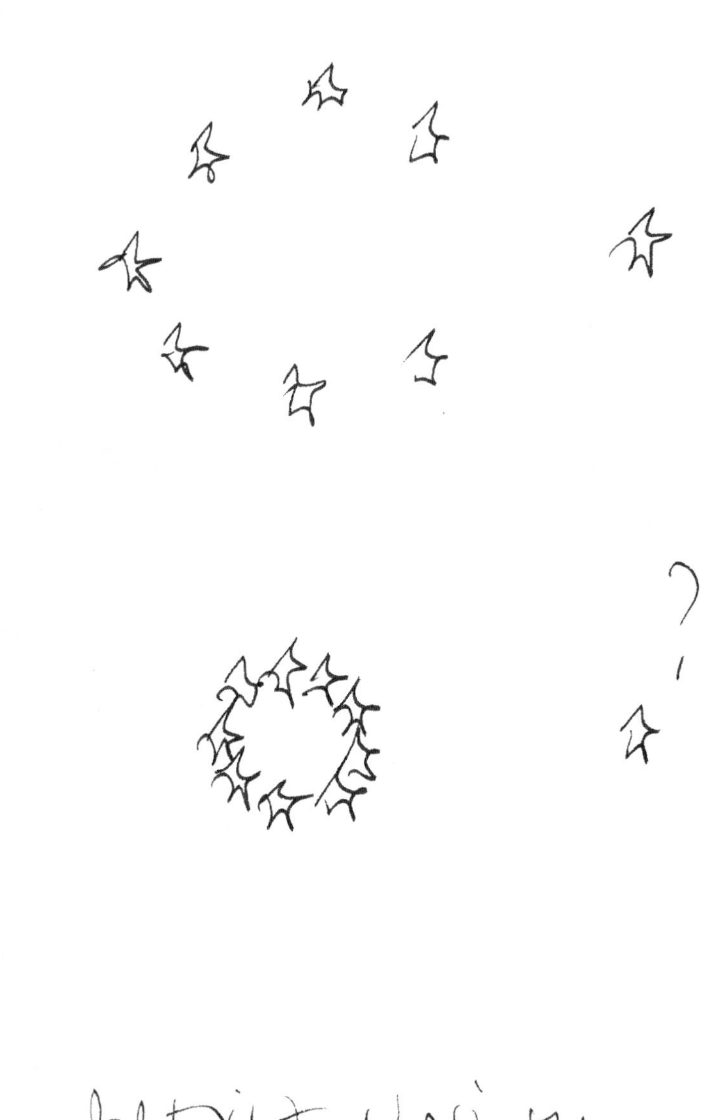

BREXIT UNITY

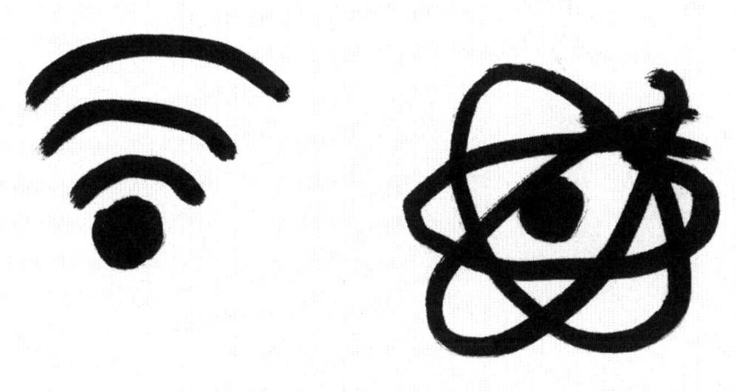

NUKE

trident

HEI CHECK MAT E

DER NEUE
SPITZ'.

where's
the
bomber?

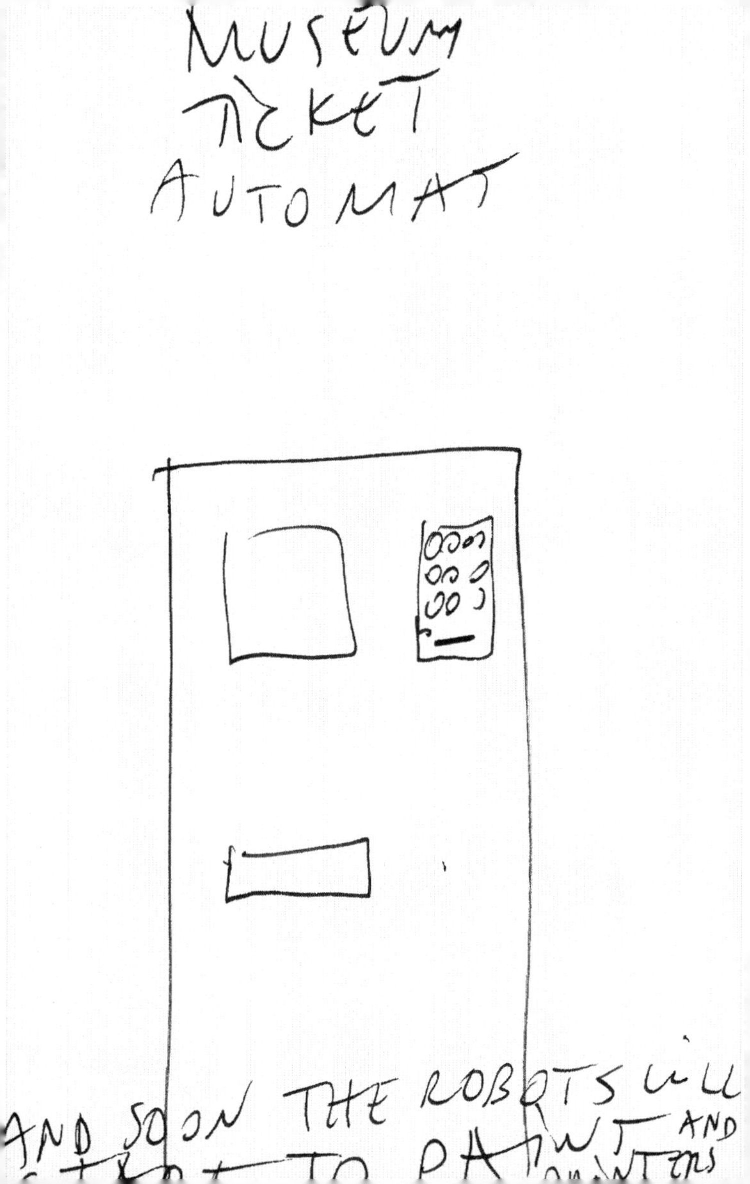

MUSEUM
TICKET
AUTOMAT

AND SOON THE ROBOTS WILL
... TO PAINT AND
PAINTERS

LOTS OF
BODIES

SURREALISM

ALMOST
NO BODY

CONTEMPORARY

well N.
I'm WRONG
THERE'S A LOTS
OF
comics SCHOOLS

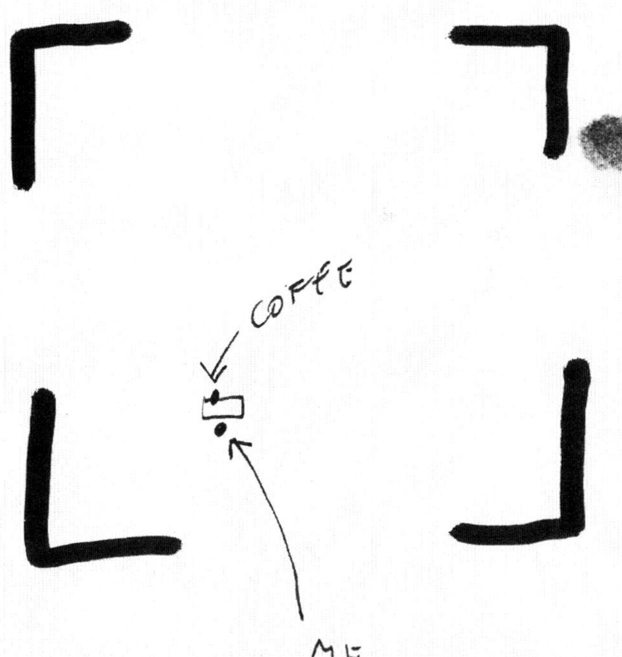
ART SPACE
COFEE
MF

SYRIAN TO
SYRIAN

3 REFUGEES ~~ARREST~~ GOJ
A TERRORIST

GOOD
SYRIAN

BAD
SYRIAN

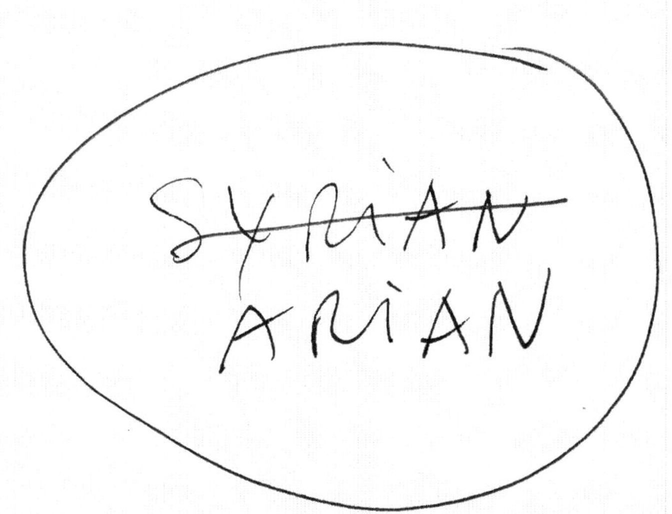

GALAXY
IS KAPUT

SAMSUNG

WE USE TO BE
UNIVERSAL
NOW WE
ARE JUST
GLOBAL

TRUMP IN THE LOCKER

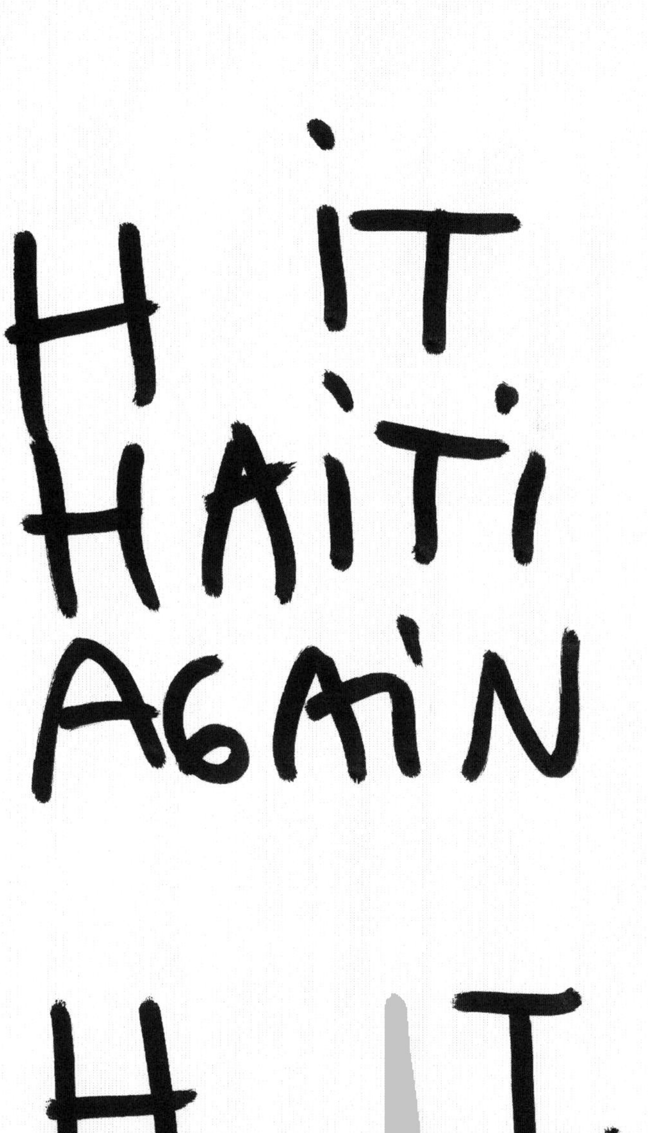

H
IT
HAITI
AGAIN
HAIT

PAZ
BY DORIS SALCEDO
BOLIVAR PLAZA
BOGOTA

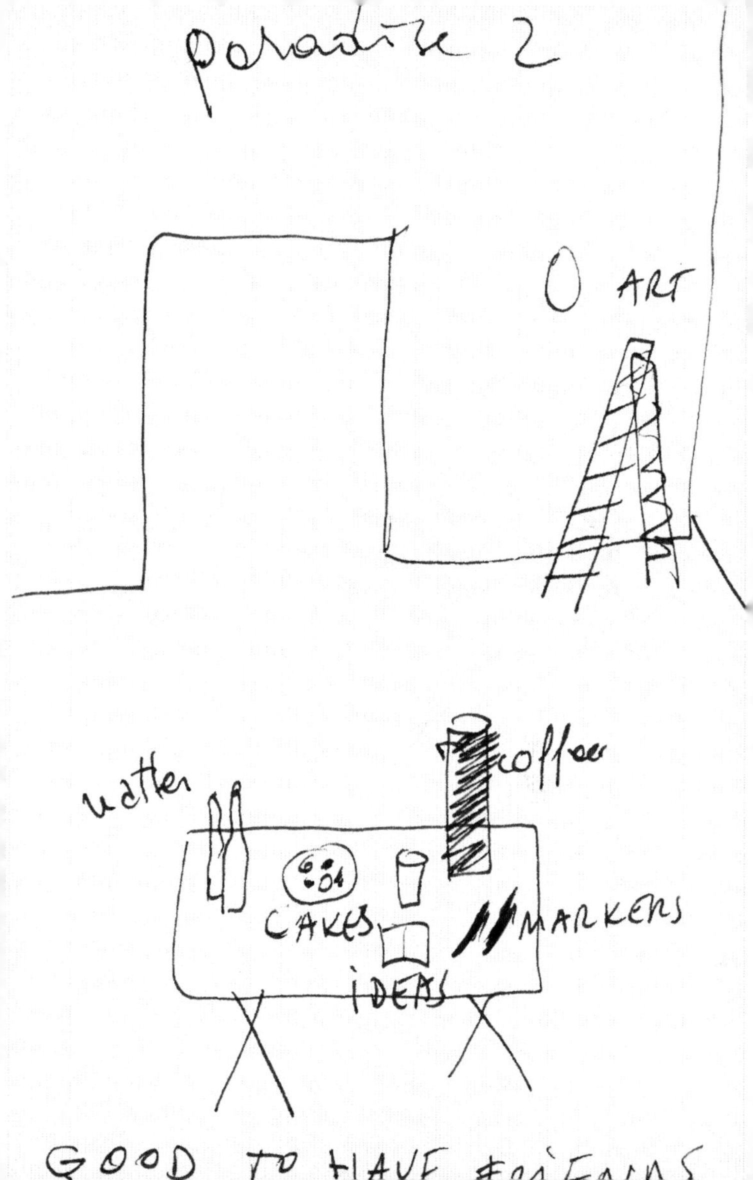

paradize 2
ART
coffee
water
CAKES
IDEAS
MARKERS
GOOD TO HAVE friends

#prize

WE ARE
GETTING
CLOSE TO
THE 30ti's.

THE 2030

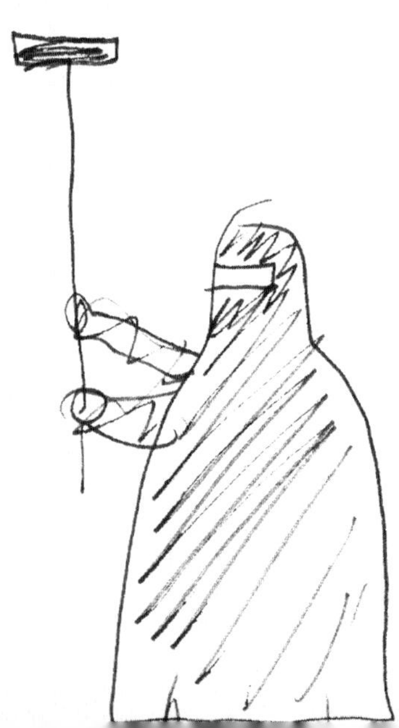

RICH
NATION
BROKEN
JEANS

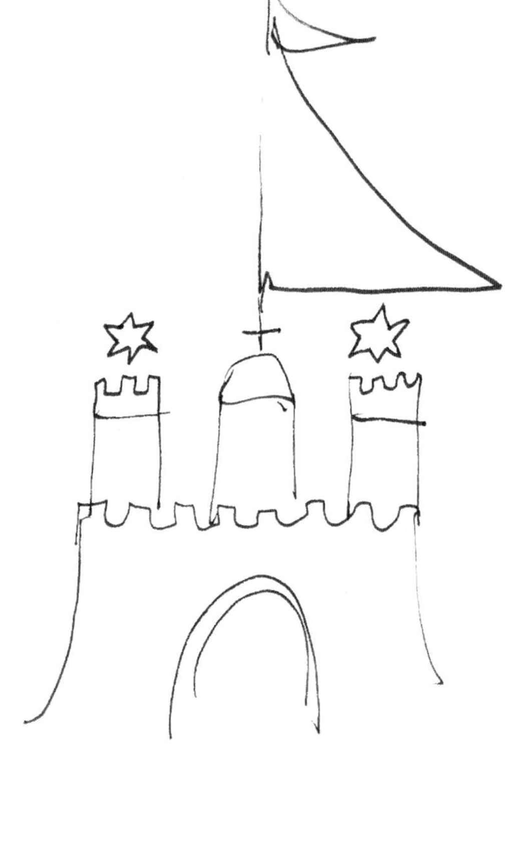

LOGO

KÜNSTLERHAUS
GALLERIES

KUNSTHAUS   KUNSTVEREIN

DEICHTORHALLEN

TITE KUNST
MILE

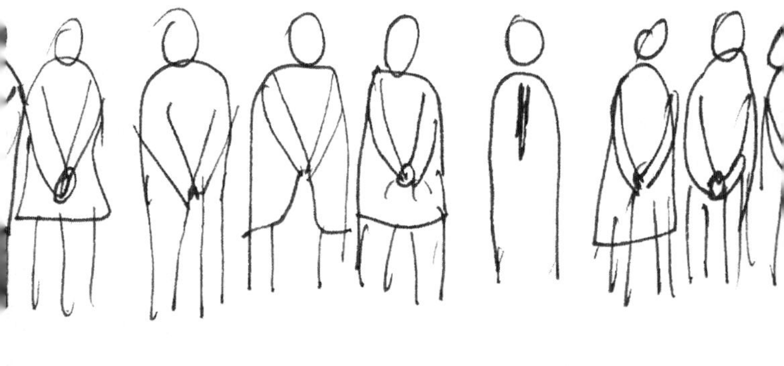

TRUMP

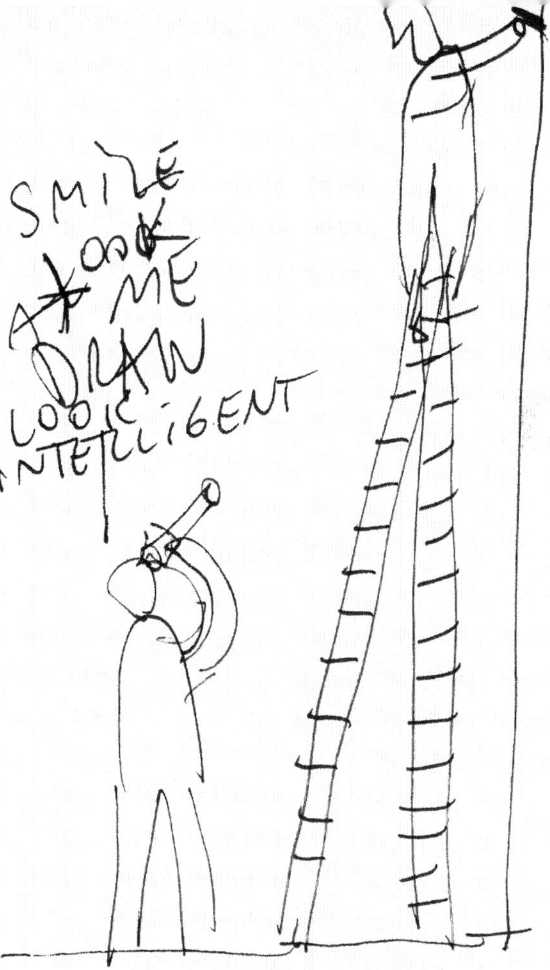

SMILE
LOOK
AT ME
DRAW
LOOK
INTELLIGENT

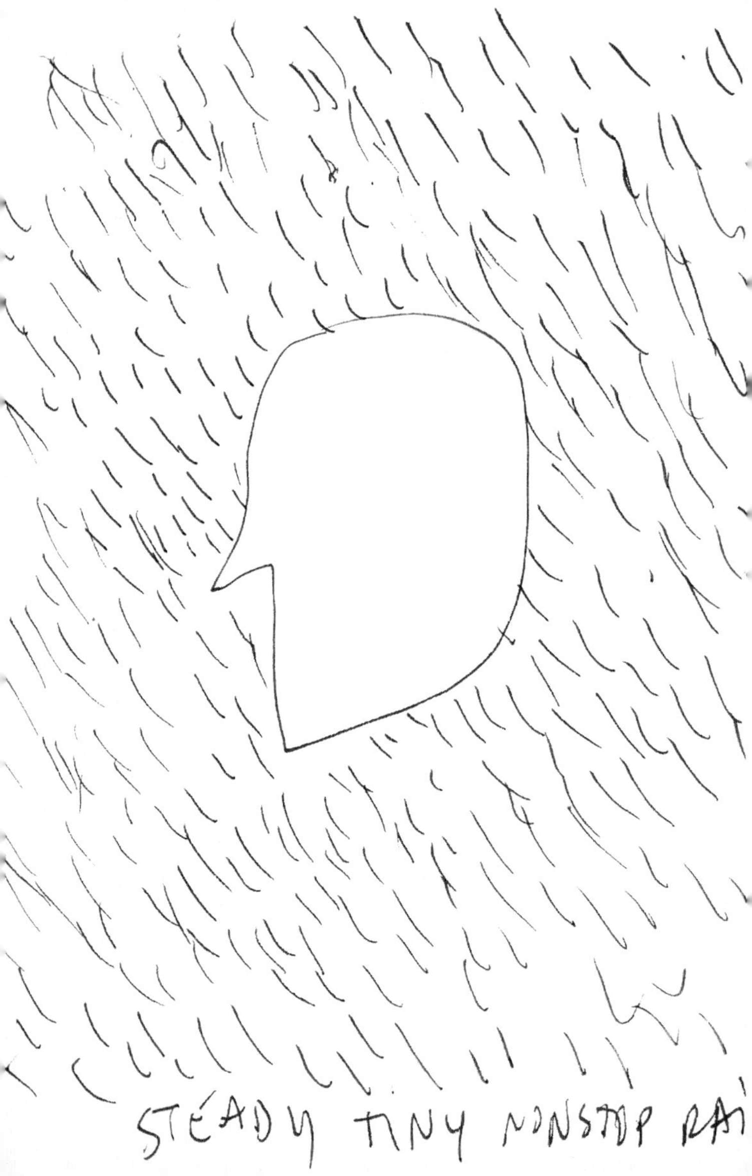

STEADY TINY NONSTOP RAI

WINTER
is
Coming

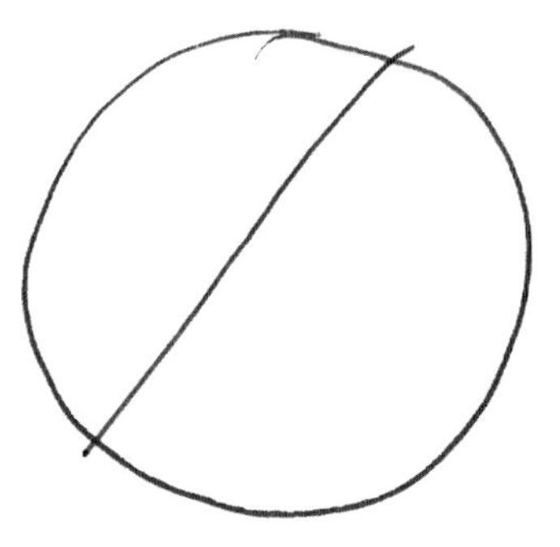

SOMETHING IS
FORBITEN

NE
ME

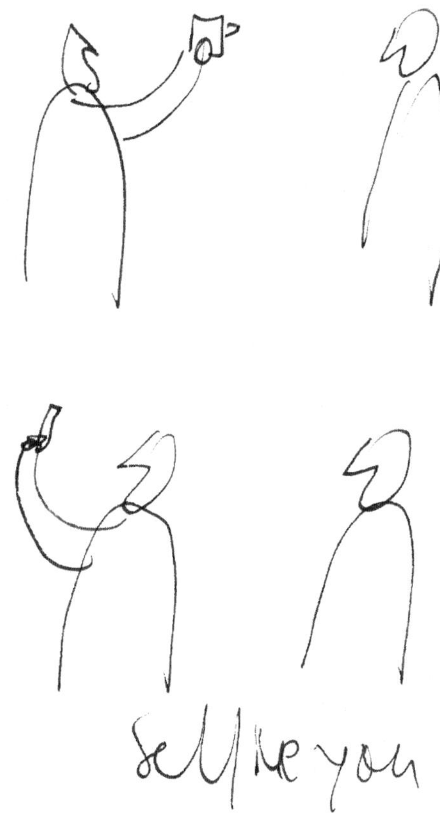

self like you

ene NO FIT

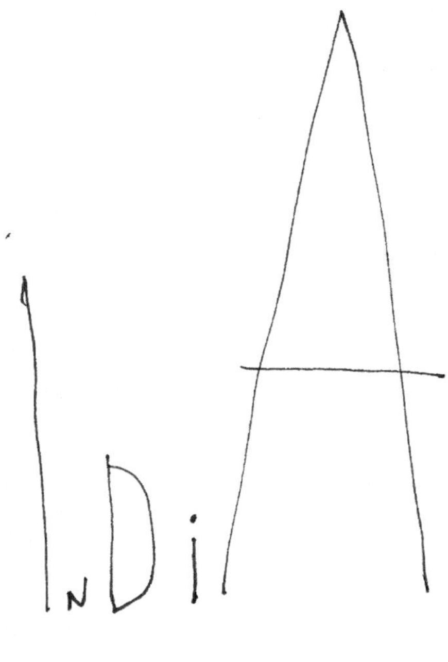

INDIA
CLASSES

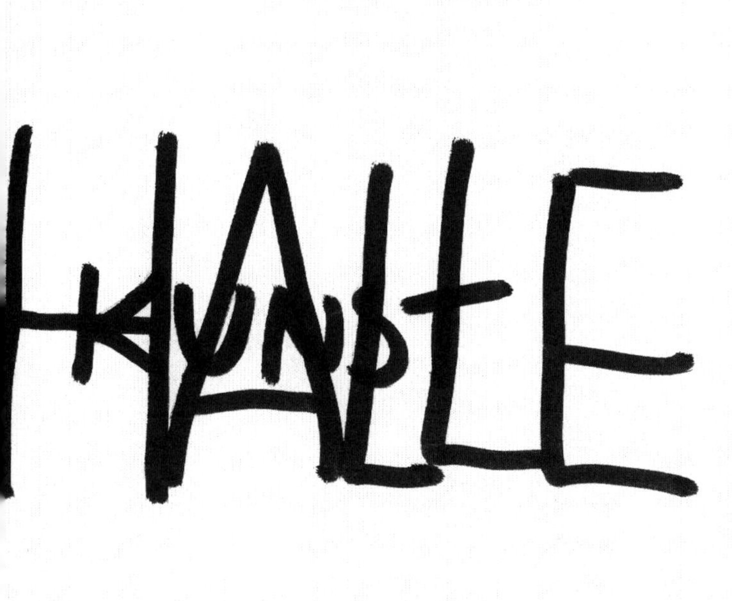

HALLE

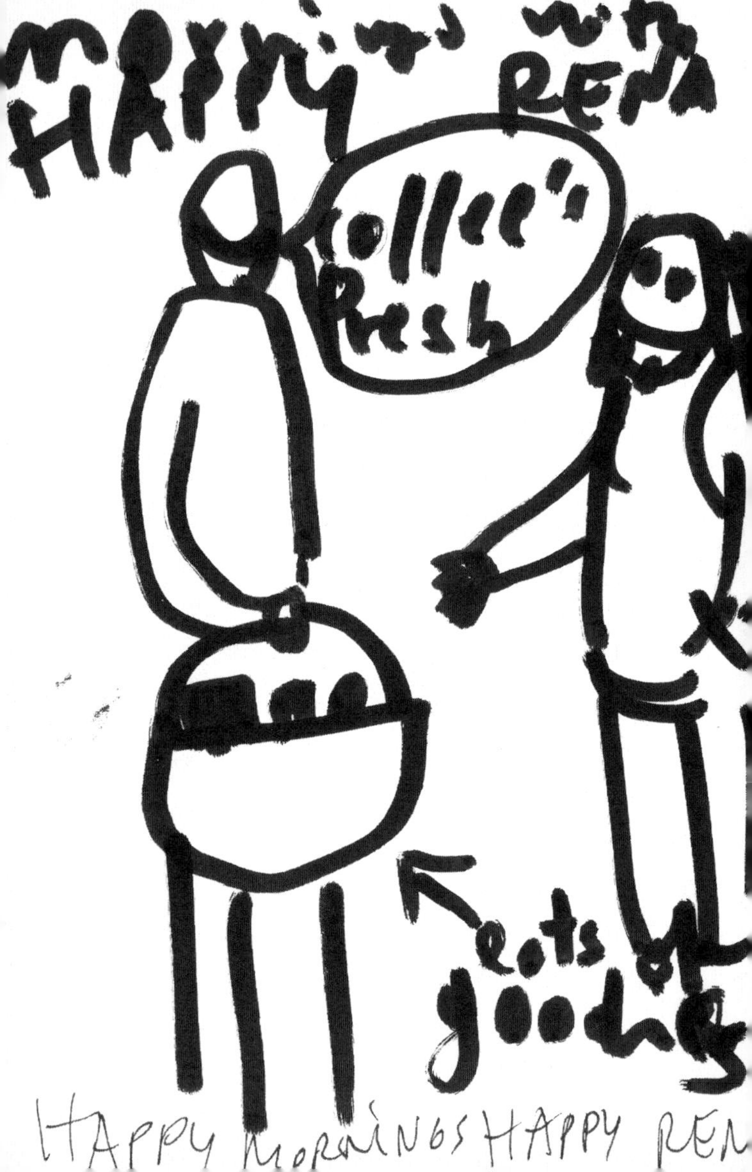

HAPPY MORNING REM
"coffee"
fresh
eots
goodes
HAPPY MORNINGS HAPPY REM

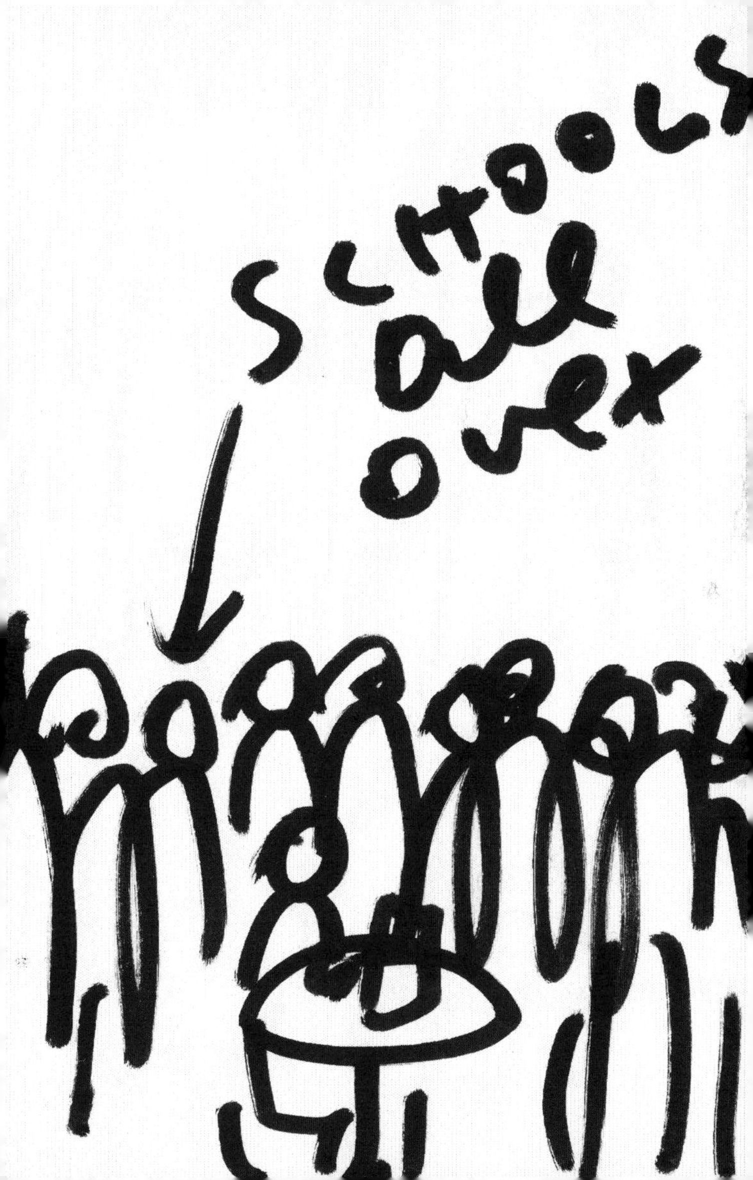
school's all over

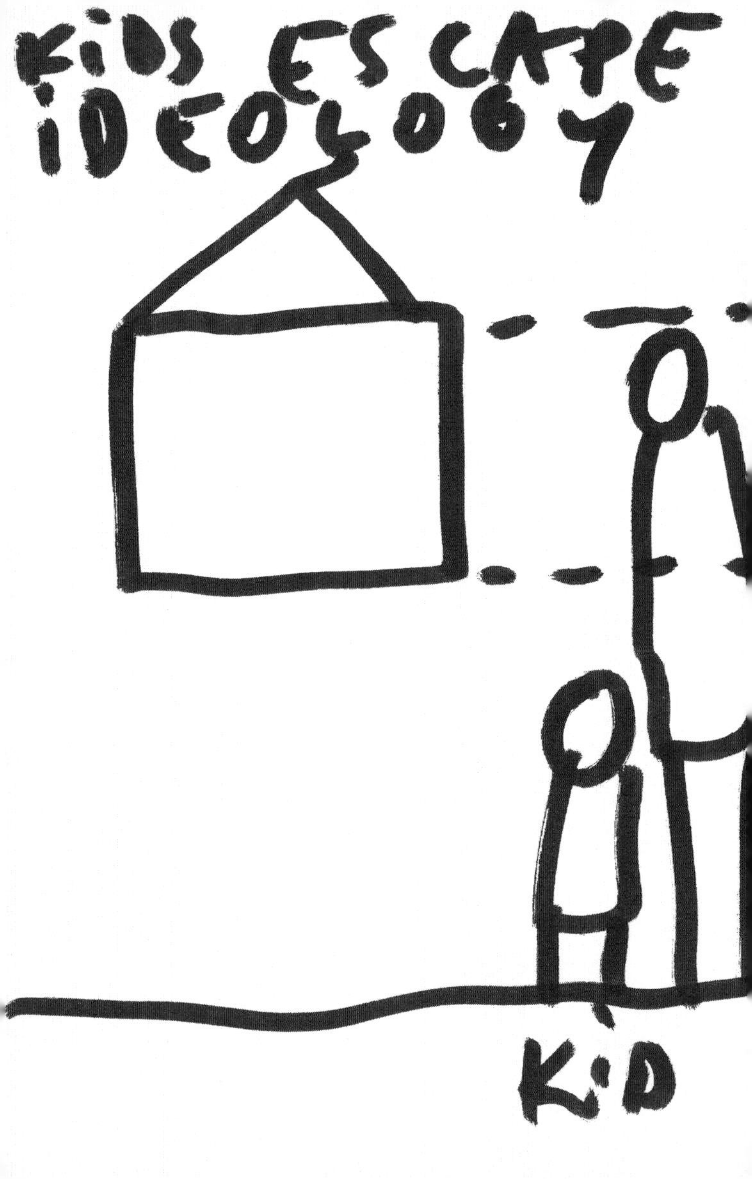

KIDS ESCAPE IDEOLOGY
KID

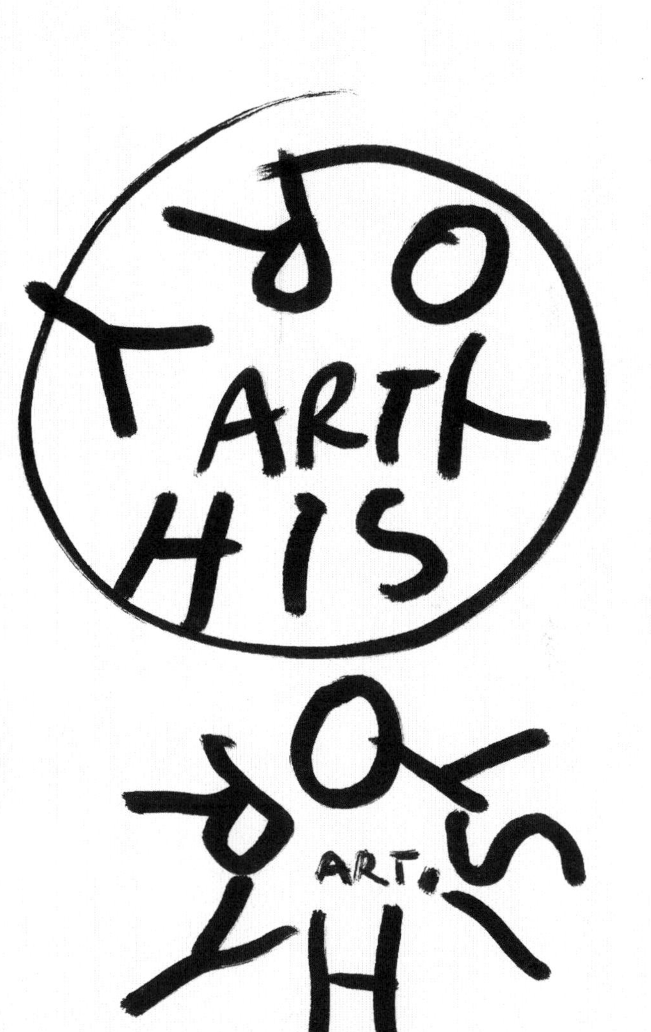
THIS
ART
HIS
ART

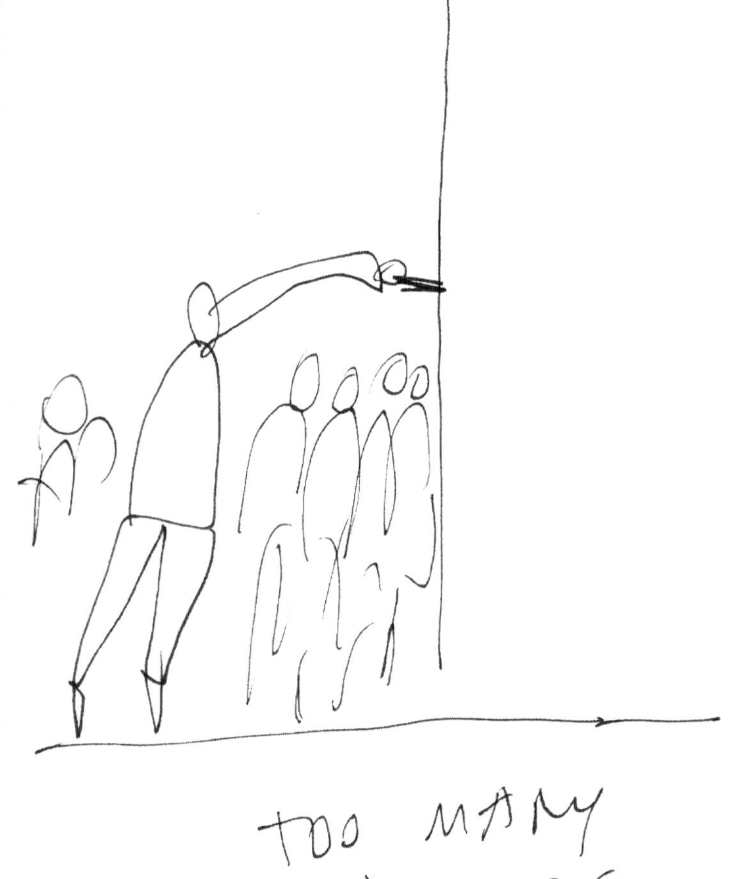
TOO MANY
VISITORS...

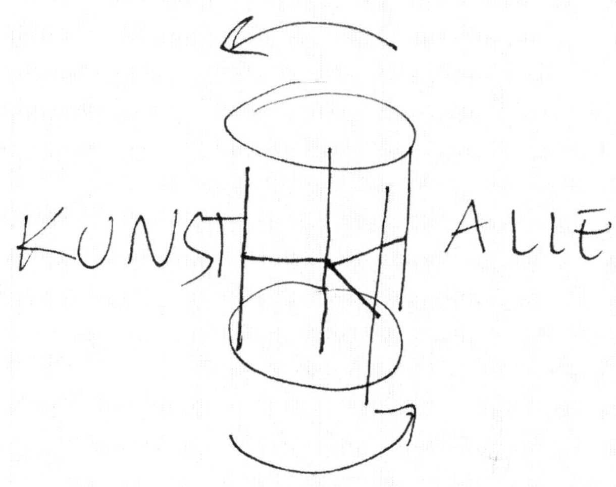
KUNSTHALLE

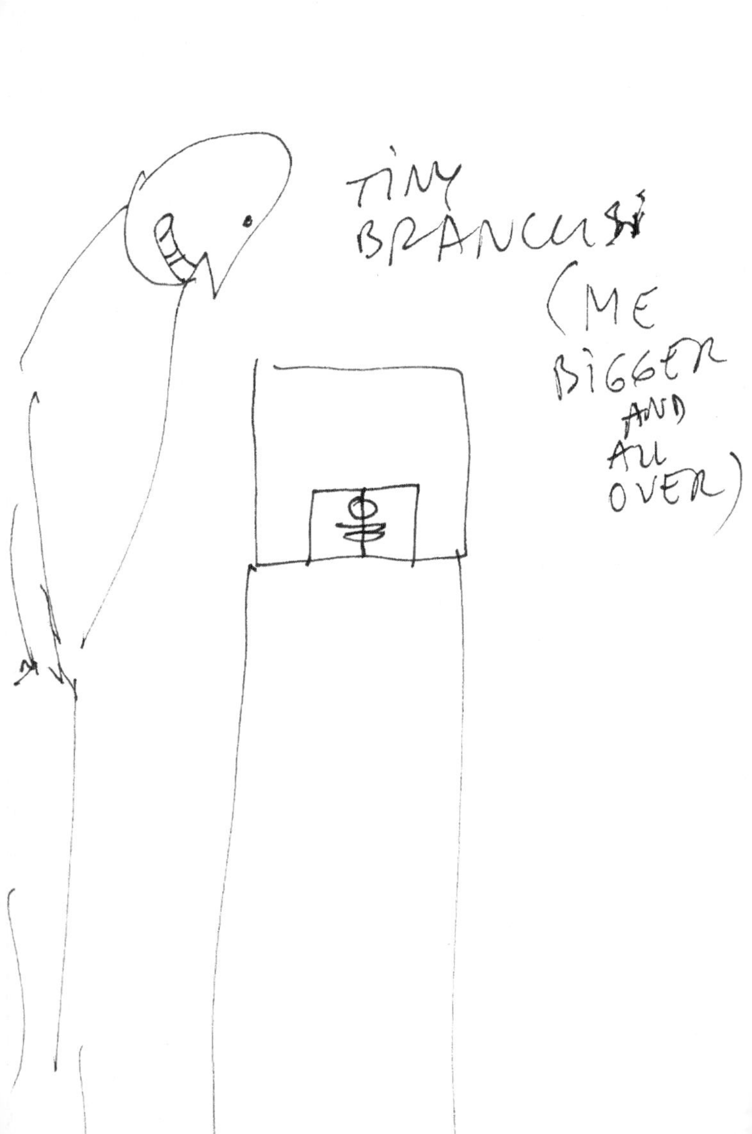

TINY
BRANCUSI
(ME
BIGGER
AND
ALL
OVER)

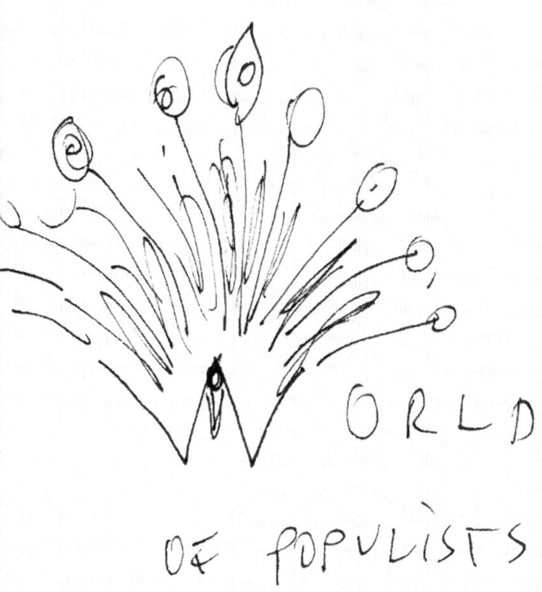

WORLD
OF POPULISTS

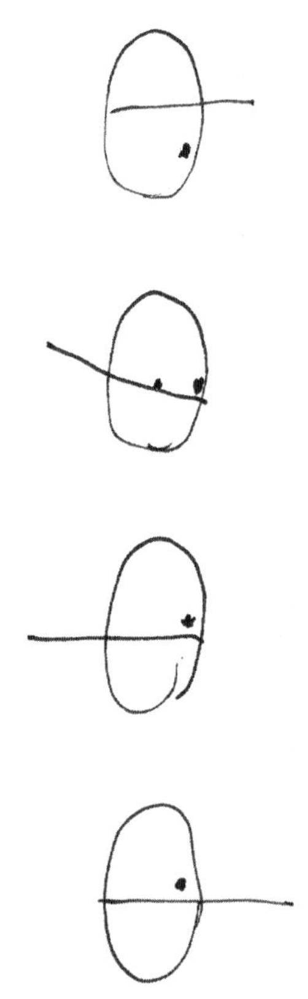

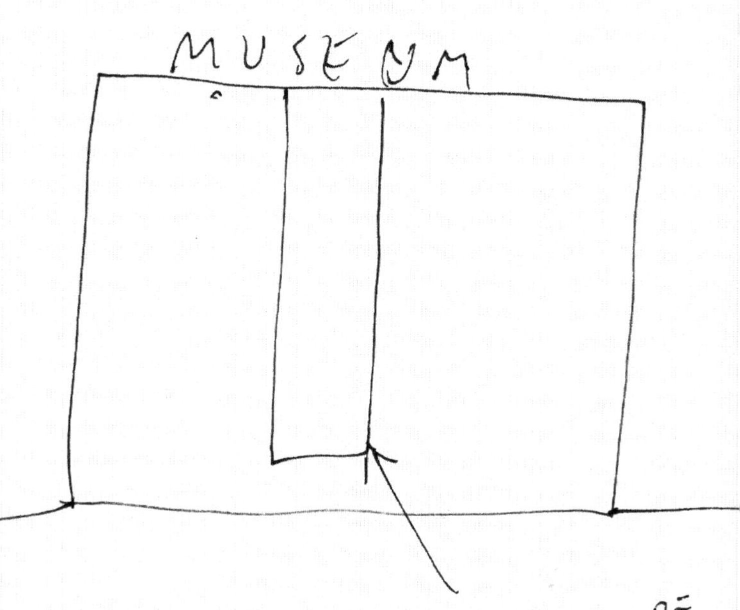

MUSEUM
POSTER OF
OTHER

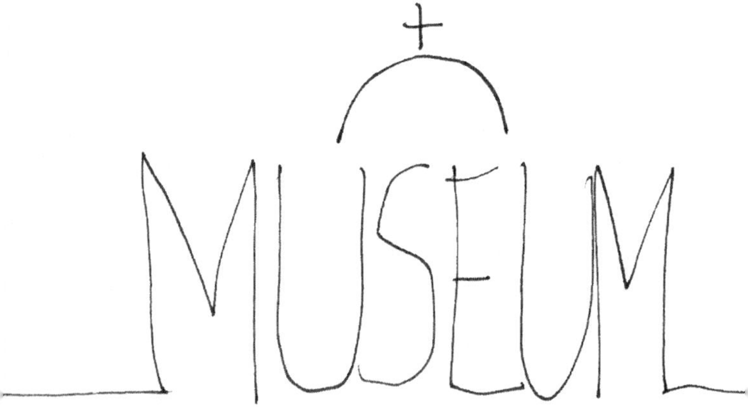

MUSEUM

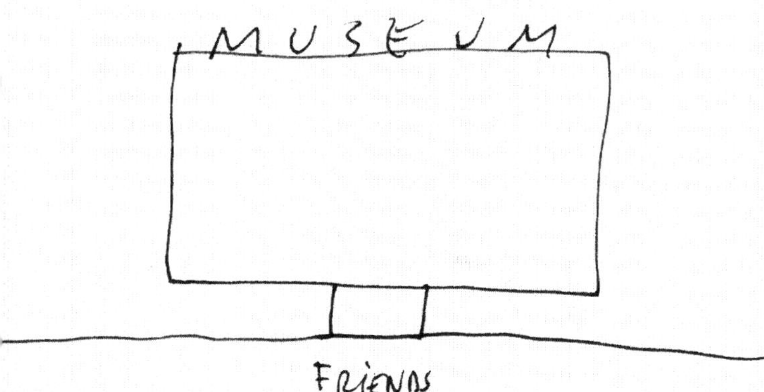
MUSEUM
FRIENDS

ENTRANCE

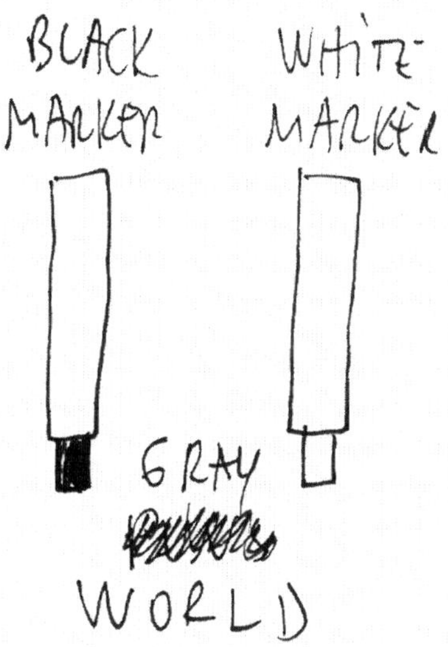

BLACK MARKER
WHITE MARKER
GRAY
WORLD

DIRECT

TRUMP

REPU|LSIVE BLICAN

TRUMP
REPUBLICAN

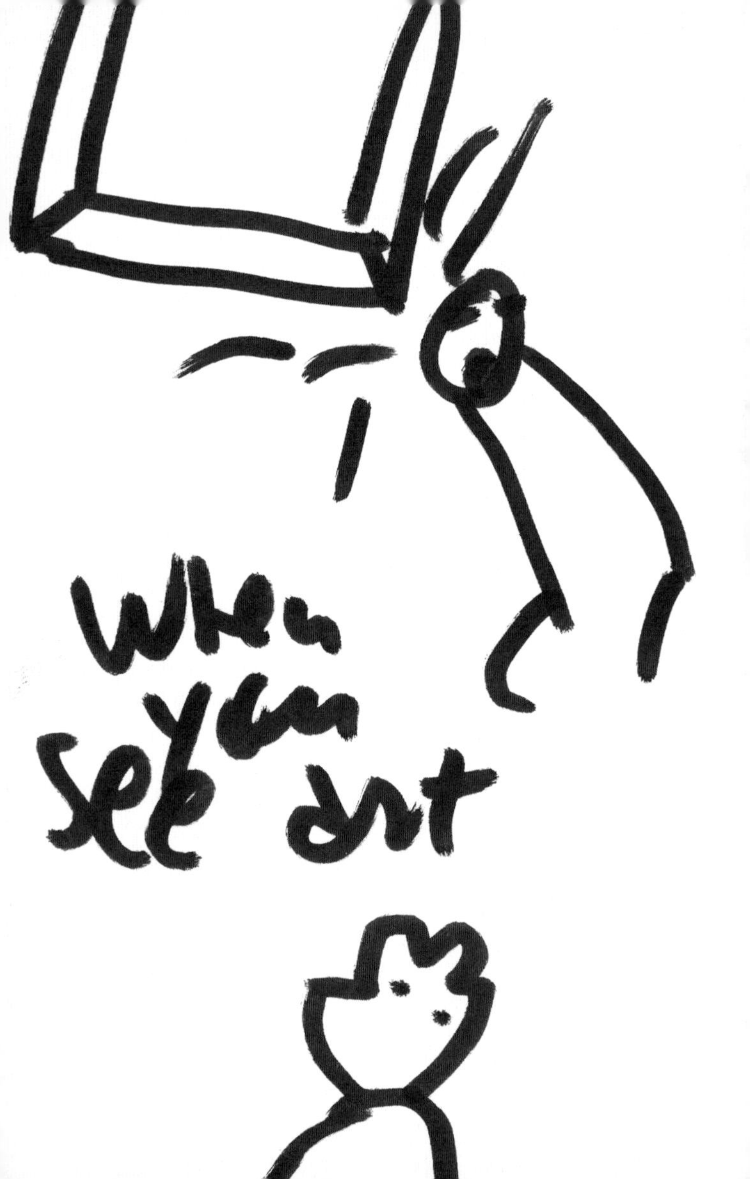
when
you
see art

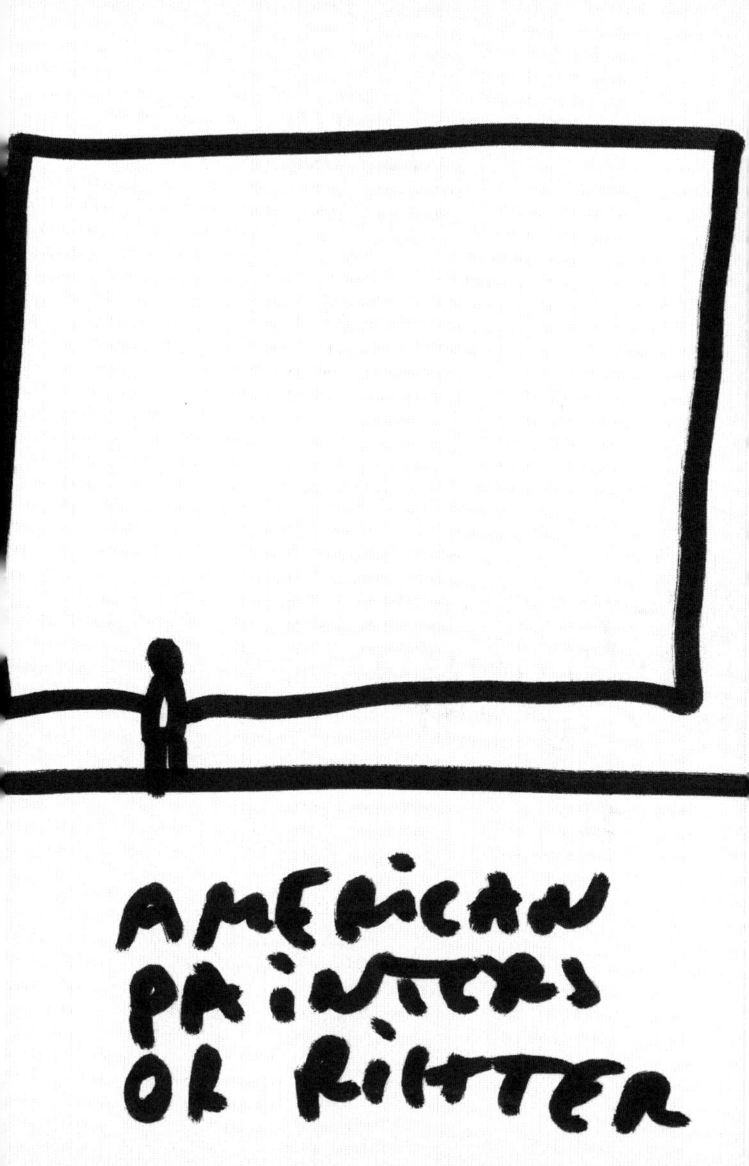

AMERICAN
PRINTERS
OR RICHTER

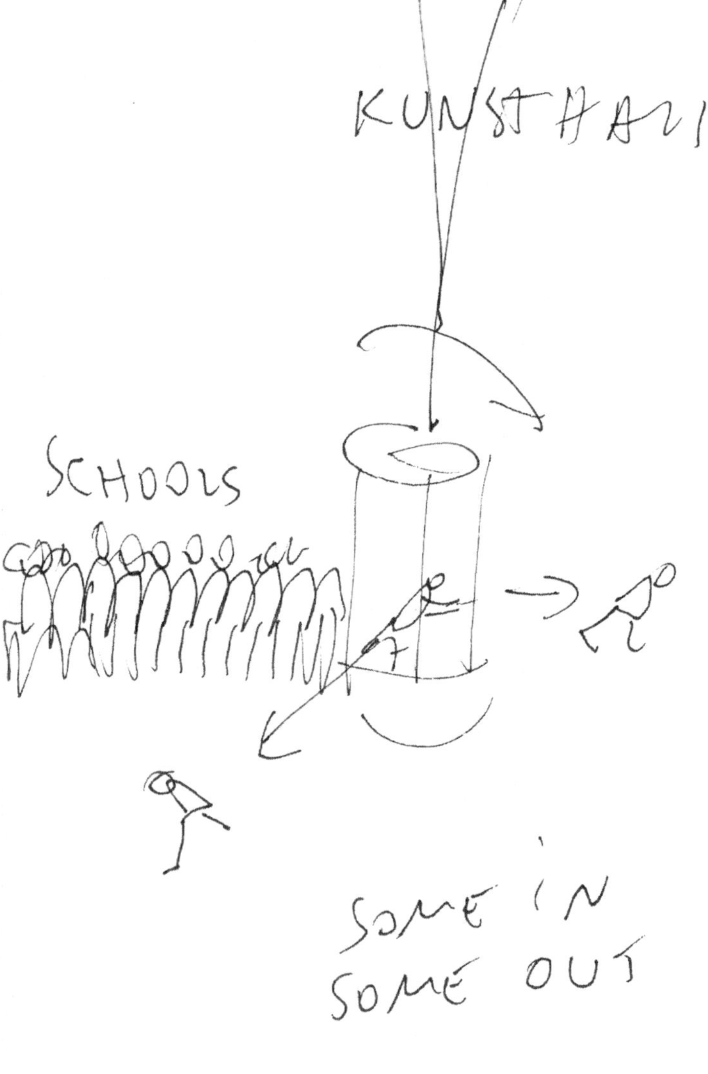
KUNSTHAL
SCHOOLS
SOME IN
SOME OUT

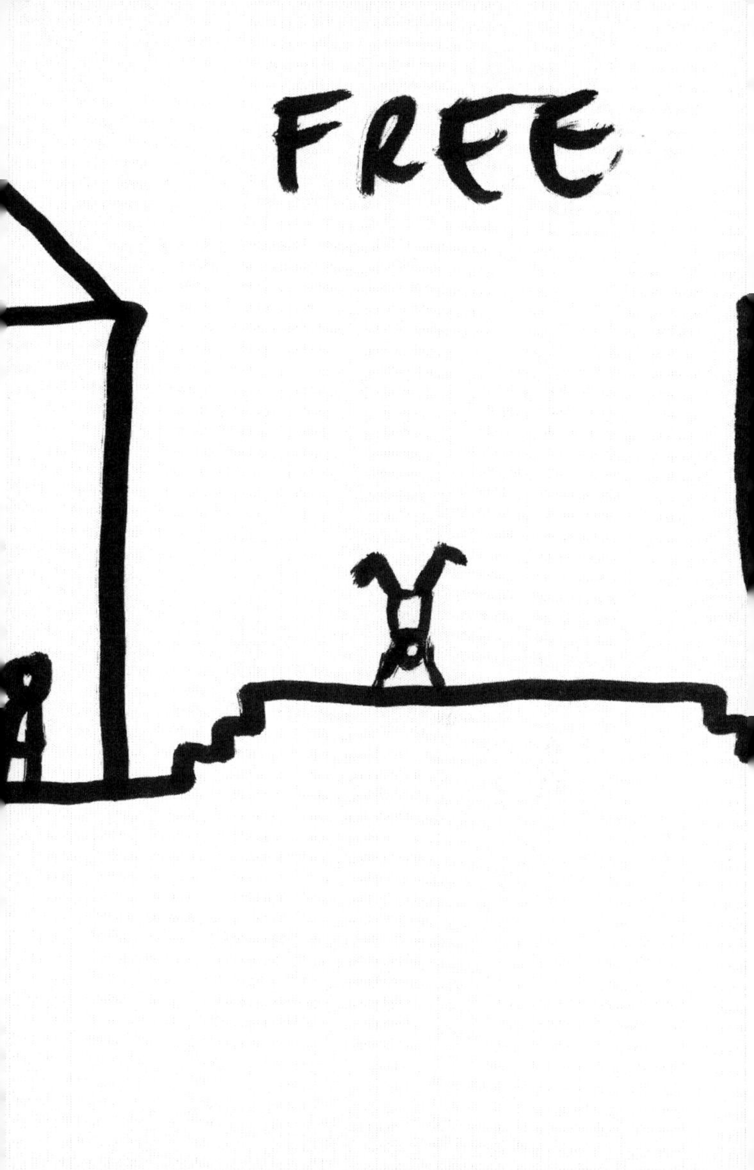

FREE

WHAT YEAR
A
WANTED ...

USORNISM

CENTRAL P
EUROPE
...
EXALT
RGHT

imPREsionir

CUBism

EXPRESionisn

OPULISM

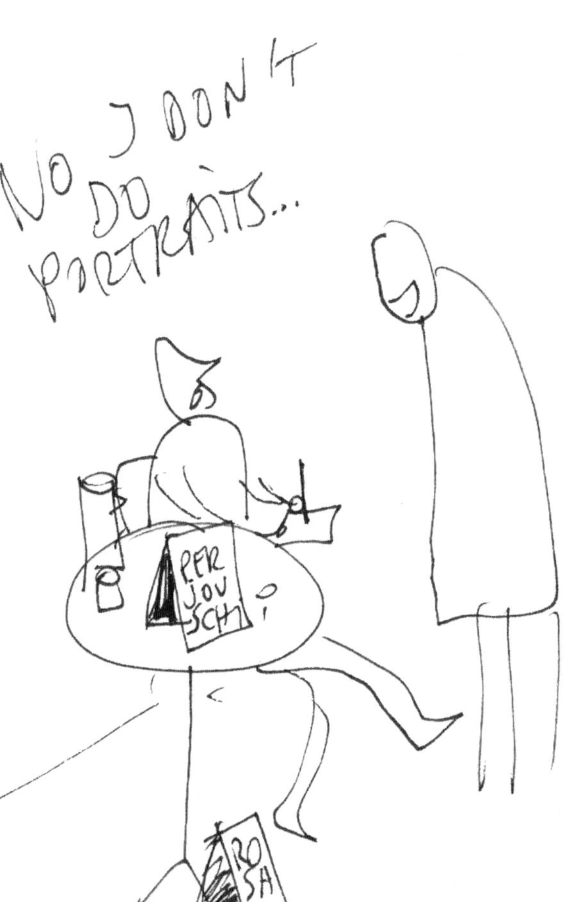

NO J DON'T
DO
PORTRAITS...
PER
JOU
SCH
B
ROSA

THE BLACK BOARDS
J PRODUCED IN
SERBIA THIS
NOTEBOOK IS
FROM CROATIA My
GALERIST IS SLOVEN.

IT'S SOMETHING
GOING ON
BETWEEN ME
AND YOU

GOSLAVIA

BOB

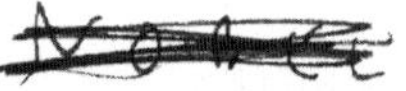

NOB EL

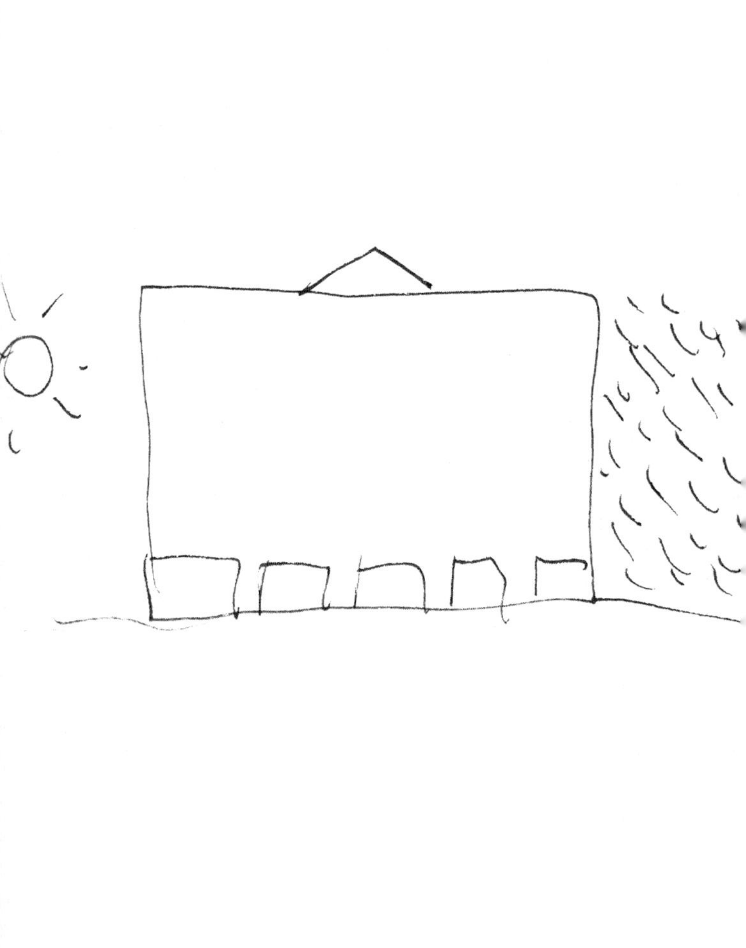

YOU
CURATOR
KUNST

Brigitte

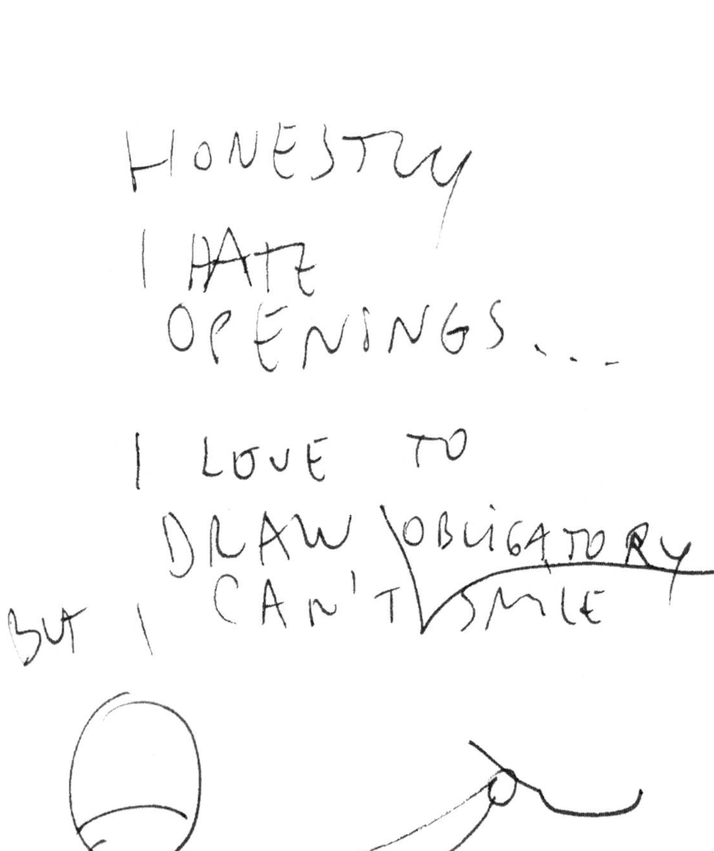
HONESTLY
I HATE
OPENINGS...

I LOVE TO
DRAW OBLIGATORY
BUT I CAN'T SMILE

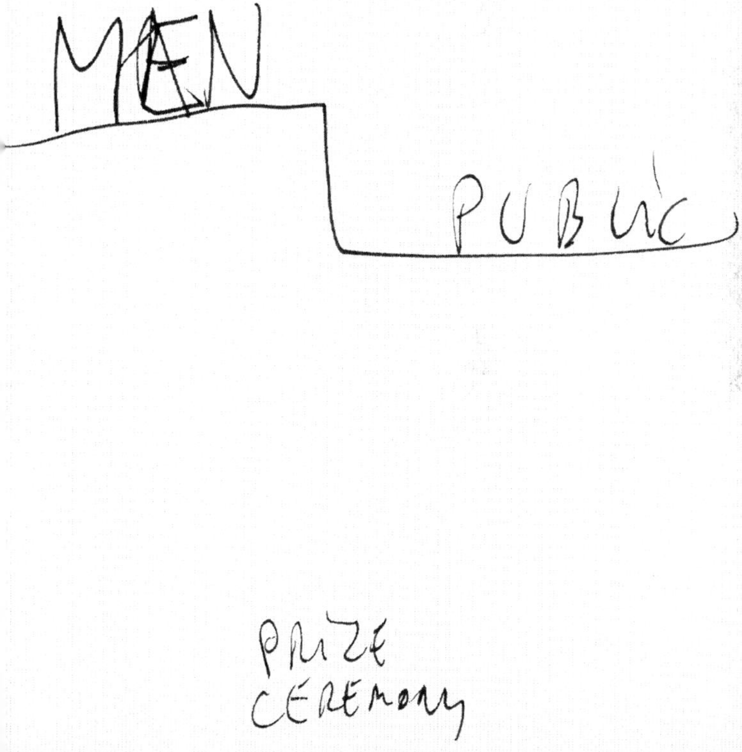

MEN
PUBLIC
PRIZE
CEREMONY

I USUALY GET PRIZES
TOGETHE WITH LIZ
PTRJOUSCM. XNITO'S
MY PARTNER IN LIFE AN
IN THINKING THE ONE
PERSON BEHIND EVERYTHIN
I DO GOOD

ROSA → NAME MCUON PUSI
② PARADOXES CONTRADICTIONS
INTELIGENT GRAFFITI
GEDANKENB
LAST TIME
I WAS ON A STAGE
WITH KASPER KOENIG
WAS IN SANKT PETERSBURG

BLANK
CHECK (CRISIS)

I LOVE MUSEUMS AND A
KUNSTVEREINS A
KUNSTHALL
MY MAIN GALLERY IS
GREGOR PODNAR
DONATION OF HALF NOTEBO

- I GOT A CALL IN A ③
BUS ... KASPER KÖNIG

- BABIAS WALDVOGEL

- KASPER KOENIG ESSEN
  KÖLN
  FRIENDS OF MUSEUM FIRST MUSEUM
- Dr. NÜMANN / DR ERGELET
- Brigitte Kolle

- LPA

- repeat the morning
  coffee water and cakes
  who must for us in
  the lobby they the RENA
  30 PER YEAR
- IN 27 YEARS 1 DID
- 60 SHOWS - KUNSTVEREIN
  STABILIZATION FESTIVAL
  STADTKURATOR

THE YEAR OF PRIZES

- ROMANIA CULTURAL JUX MUNDI
  SPECIAL PR
- PRIZE ~~FELLOWSHIP~~ ACTIVST NATIONAL PLATFO-
  CERE (CITIZEN)

- AND NOW ROOT

  CITIZEN AND ARTIST

CURATOR
KUNST
KUNST
CURATOR

ROSA WAS COOL

AND TO THAT ASIAN LOOKIN
SUPERVIZOR WHO ENJOY SO MUCH
SOME OF MY DRAWINGS WAS

SOME MONTH AGO A PHONE IN THE BUS
IT SARTED LONG TIME
AGO

– BABIAS WALDVOGEL
      2003
– 2005 LUDWIG KOLM
   – FIRST WESTERN
MUSEUM AND AQUISITION

   MANIFESTA ?
–

– HAMBURG – KUNSTVEREIN
        STADTKURATORIUM

– BRIGITTE KÖLLE SUBVISION
            6+1A

THANK YOU KASPER KÖNIG
  ~~STARTED~~
        FRIENDS OF KUNSTHALLE
MR. NEUMAN DR KATRIN ERGELT
BRIGITTE – PETRA RENA

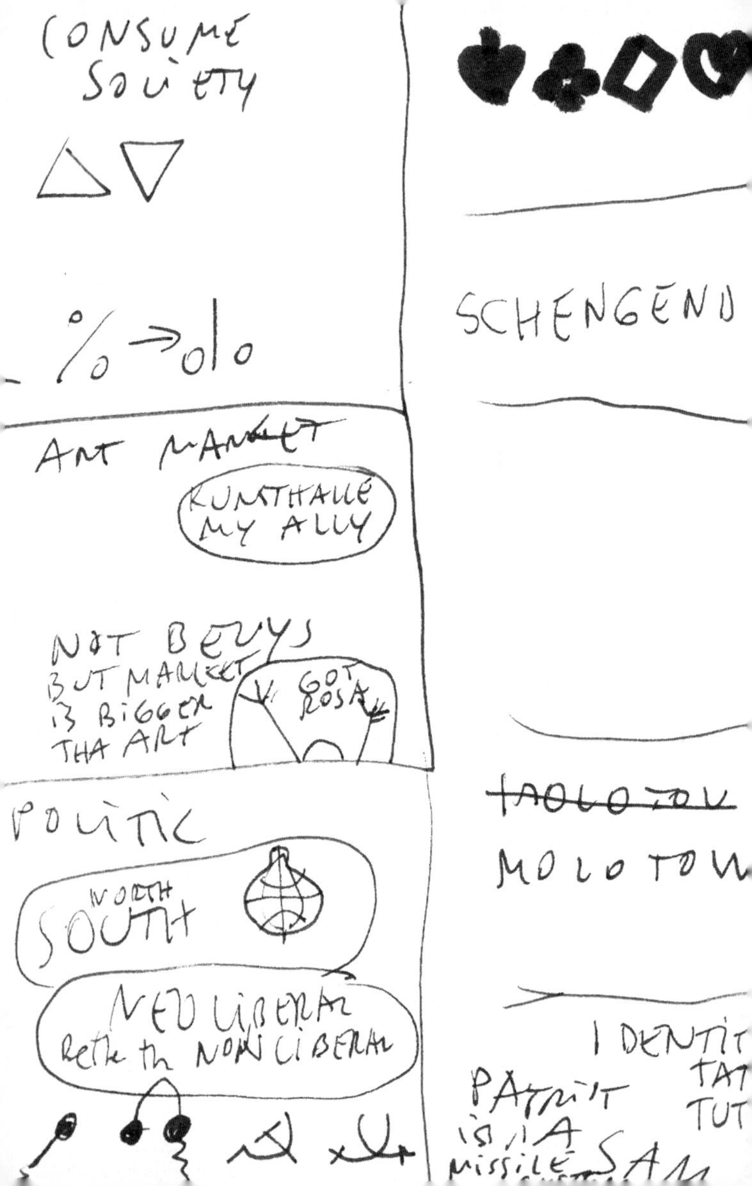

CONSUME
SOCIETY

-% → %

ART MARKET
KUNSTHALLE
MY ALLY

NOT BEUYS
BUT MARKET
IS BIGGER
THA ART

GOT
ROSA

POLITIC
NORTH
SOUTH

NEOLIBERAL
Rette th NON LIBERAL

SCHENGEN

MOLOTOV

IDENTIT
TAT
TUT
PATRIOT
IS A
MISSILE SAM

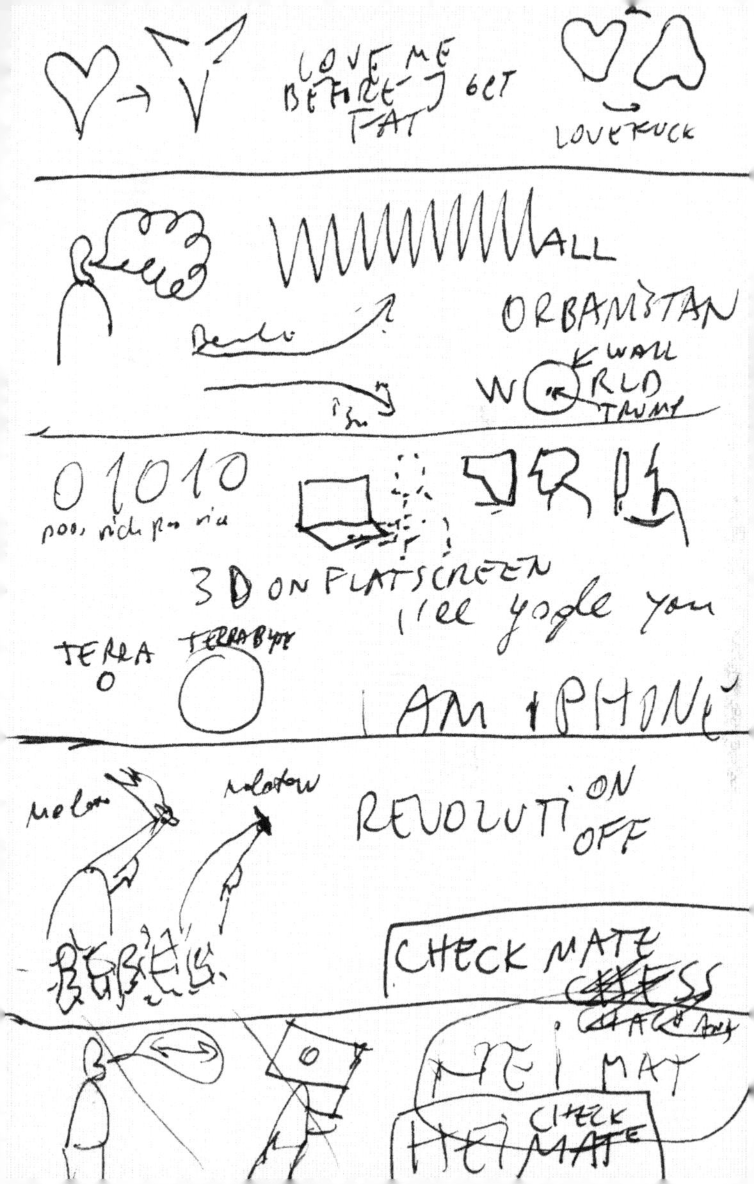

LOVE ME BEFORE I GET FAT
LOVEFUCK
WALL
ORBANISTAN
WORLD TRADE
WALL
0 1 0 1 0
poor rich poor rich
3D ON FLATSCREEN
i'll google you
TERRA O
TERRABYTE
I AM iPHONE
molon
molotow
REVOLUTION ON OFF
BABIES
CHECK MATE
CHESS
CHECK MATE
CHECK MATE

ANGST
Hilary
TRUMP
NO GRAFFITI
ON RAZOR-WIRE
WALLS
SA FAC
CEVA CU
SEMNELE
#PRIZE
HAITI
AGAIN
TRUMP
THE
LOCKE
TICKET MACHINE
AND SOON
ROBOTS
WILL
PAINT
NUKE
OLD NEW
MICHEL A
Dot vinci GUY
DALI Poster MONAL
LAMPEDUSA
VIRUSSIA

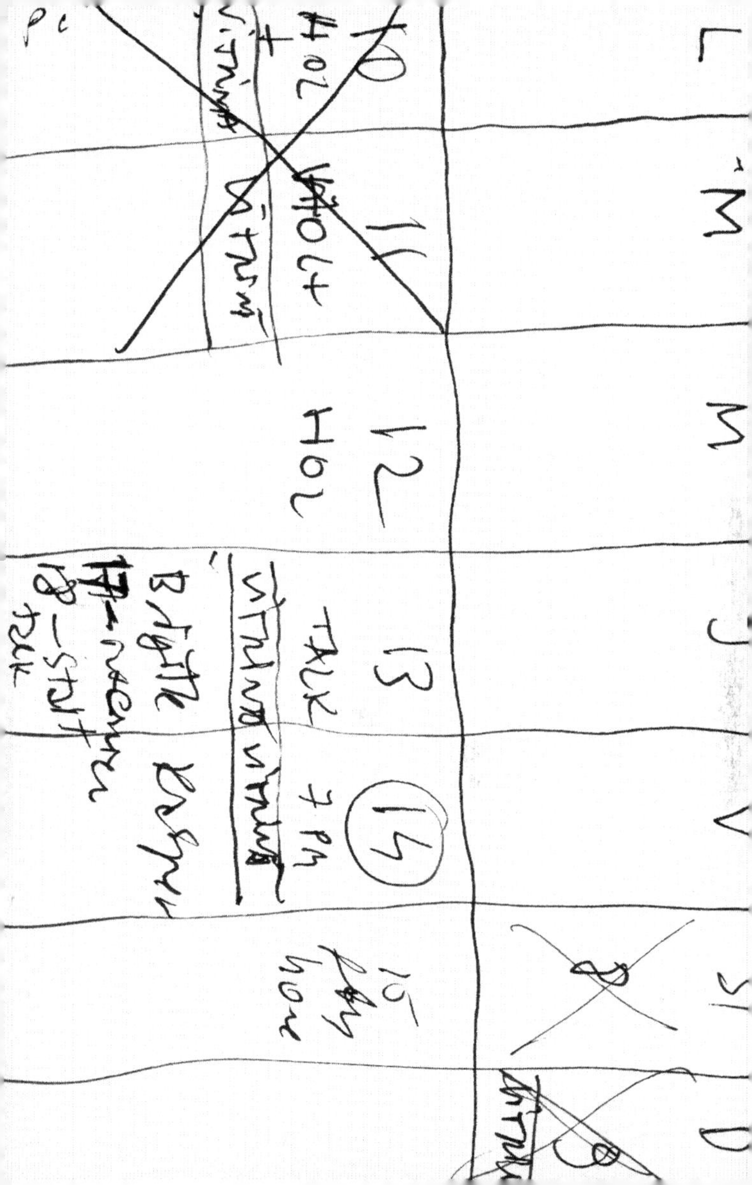

SREBRENICA
ALEPPO
HEIMAT
CHECK
ZUKUNFT
GEDANKENBILD
UST OF
KUNSTHALL
STEINWALL
LANGE MUHREN
SPITALGASSE
HBF
18/2
STEINTORDAM
ALTE STADT
MÖNCKEBERGE
KAU HOF
SATURN
ALTMANBRUCKE
HEM
STEINITRO
KUNST
BAHNHOF
K
AM
MA
SA
UA
HOTEL
A80
Reich

OSSI
WESSI
STRESSI

REAL FEIT

LEADER
DIE
DAS

DON'T SAY
THE F
WORD
FUTURE

EUROPE
PUTIN

CORNER
SELFIE

ZUKUNFT

SUBVISION

MIGRANT
MIGRENE

SCHENGEND

TRAGODY
AGODY
GODY
GOOD
ENTERTAINMENT

0049 176 50 96 25 26

HOTEL HENRI
BUGENHAGENSTRASSE 21

S1 From Airport
HBF → MÖNCKEBERGSTRASSE
CROSS → LEFT TO LANGE MÜHREN
INTO MALL   RIGHT TO BUGENHAG-

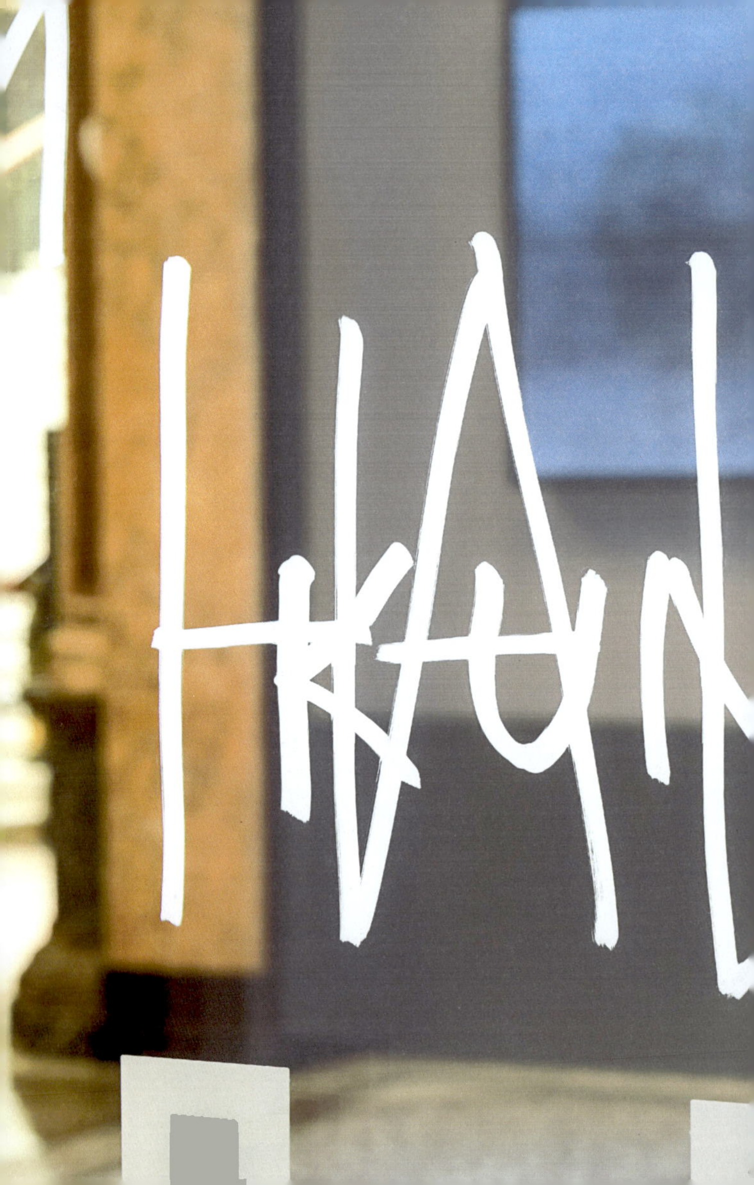

HAN
HAU

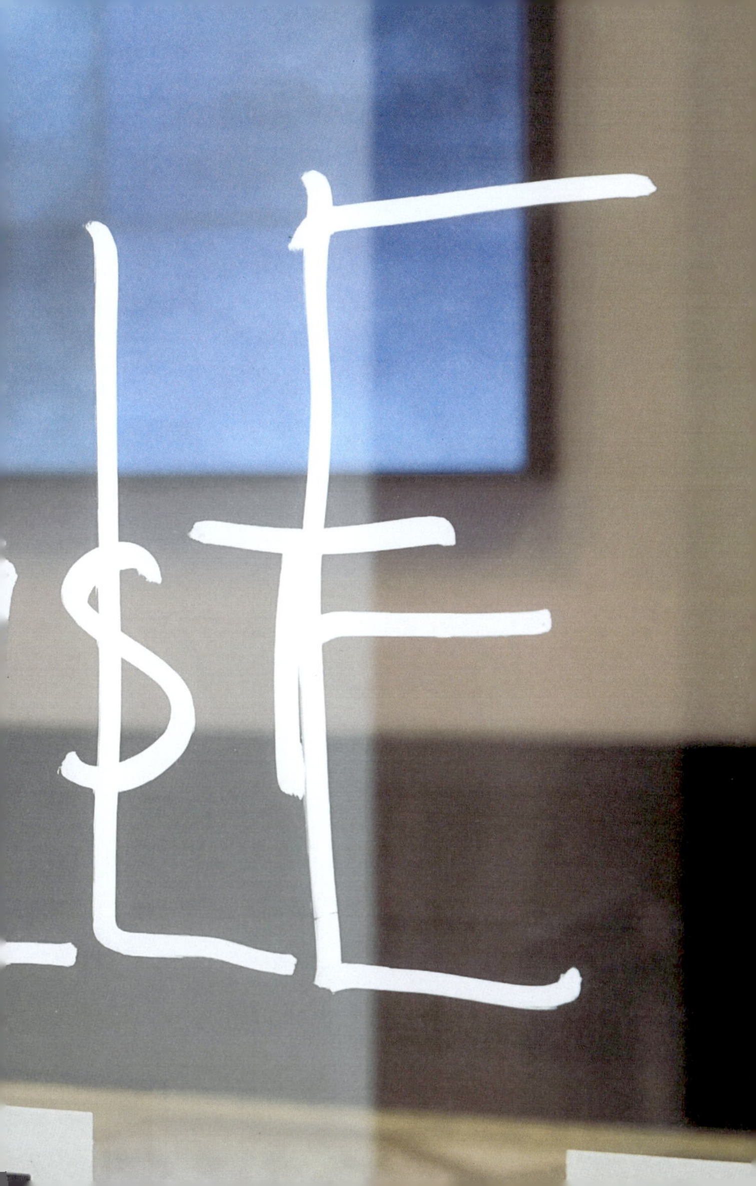

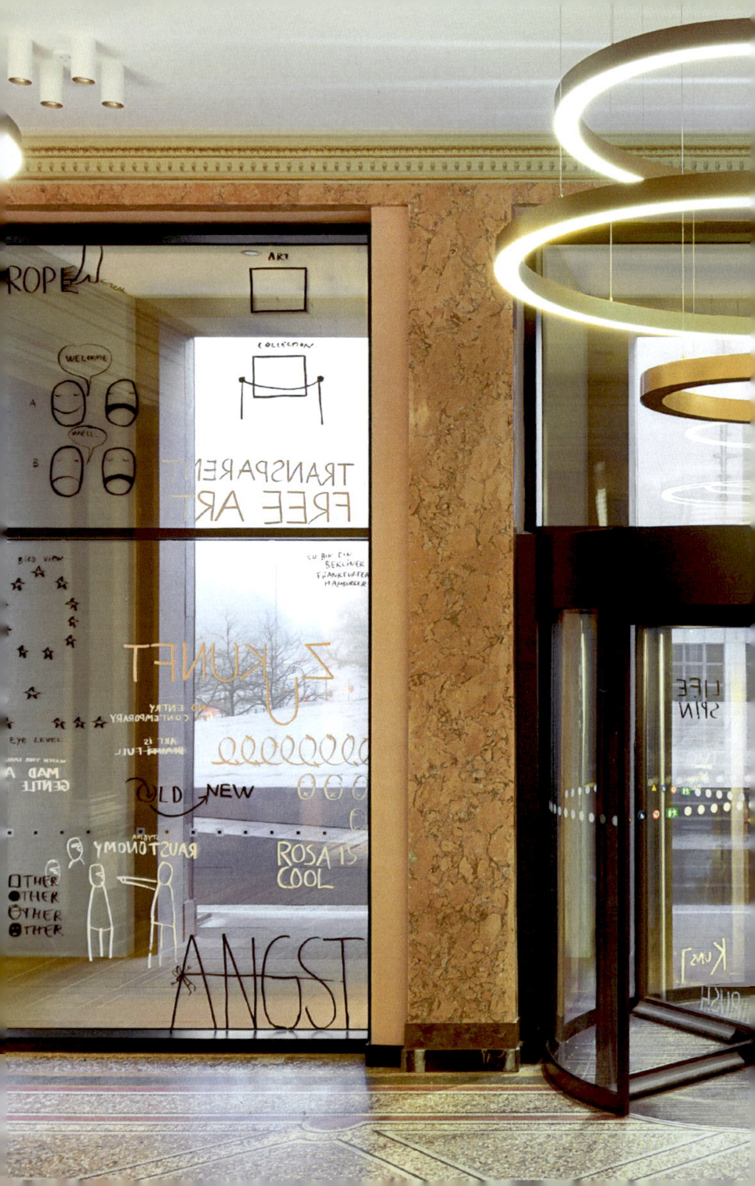
WELCOME
WELL...
A
B
COLLECTION
TRANSPARENT
FREE ART
ICH BIN EIN
BERLINER
FRANKFURTER
HAMBURGER
BIRD VIEW
ZUKUNFT
NO ENTRY
CONTEMPORARY
EYE LEVEL
ART IS
BEAUTIFUL
MAD A
GENTLE
OLD NEW
RAUSTONOMY
ROSA IS
COOL
OTHER
OTHER
OTHER
OTHER
ANGST
LIFE
SPIN
KUNST

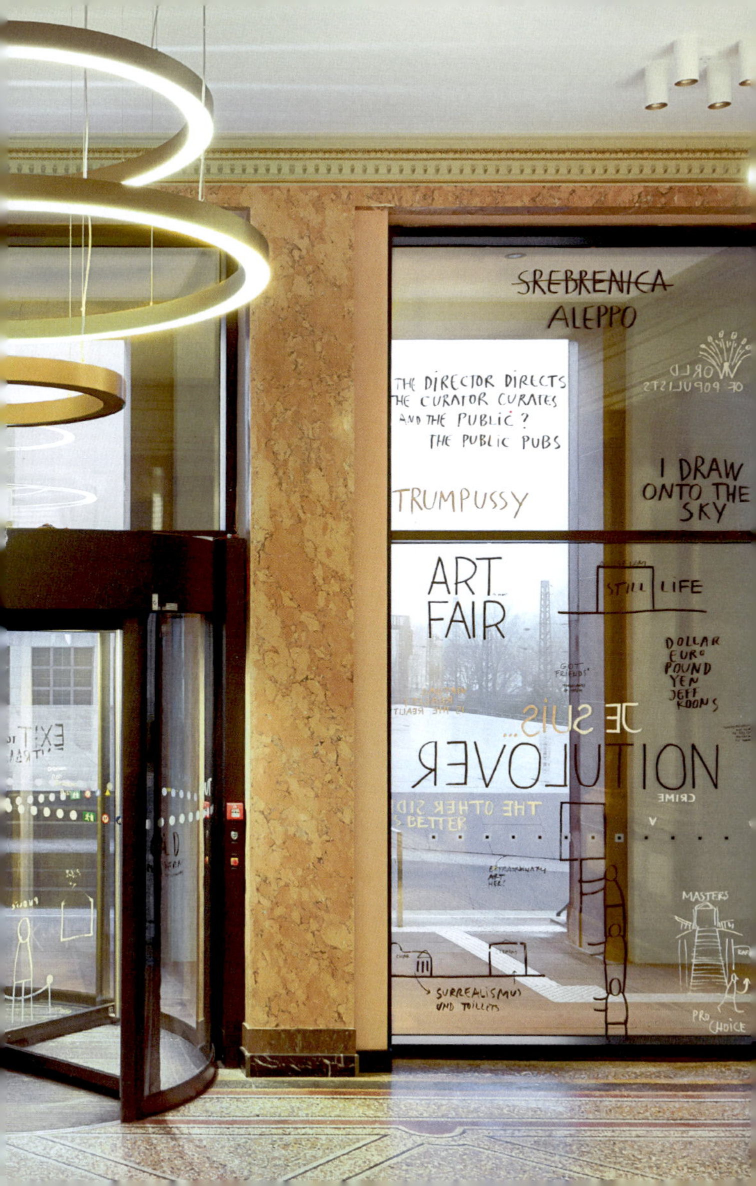

SREBRENICA
ALEPPO
THE DIRECTOR DIRECTS
THE CURATOR CURATES
AND THE PUBLIC ?
THE PUBLIC PUBS
TRUMPUSSY
WORLD OF POPULISTS
I DRAW ONTO THE SKY
ART FAIR
STILL LIFE
DOLLAR
EURO
POUND
YEN
JEFF KOONS
JE SUIS...
REVOLUTION
CRIME
MASTERS
SURREALISMUS UND TOILETS
PRO CHOICE
EXIT

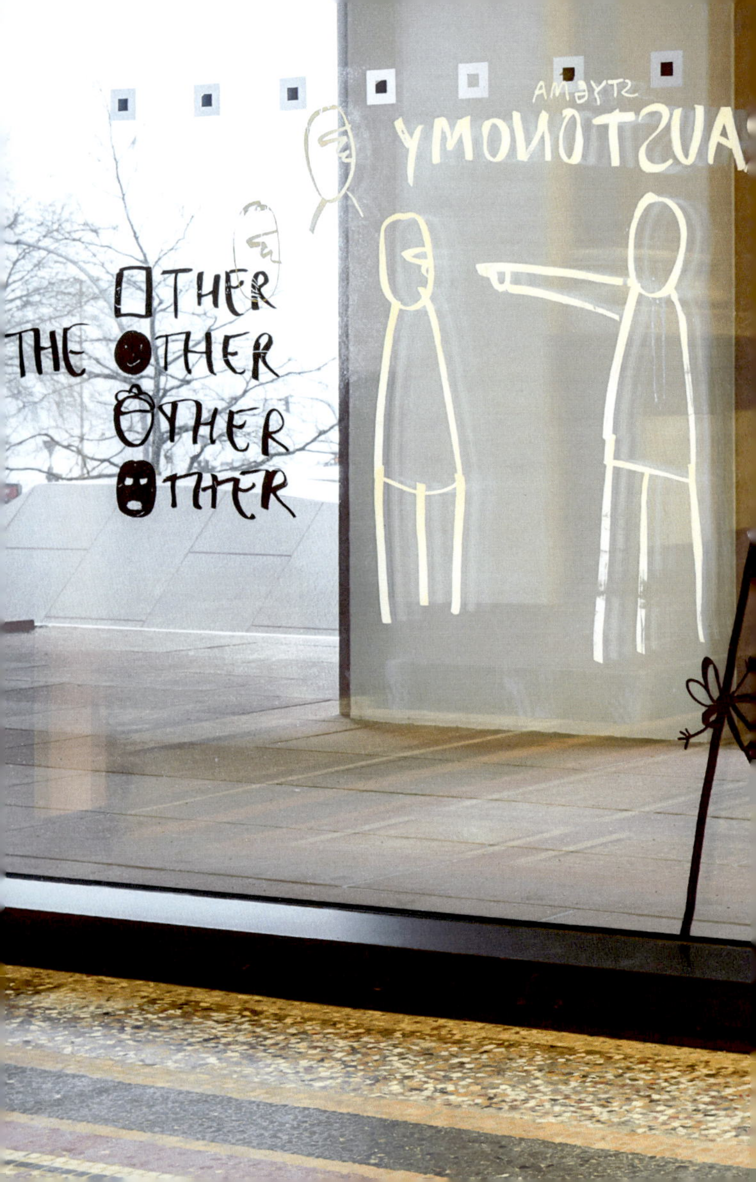

Other
THE Other Other Other

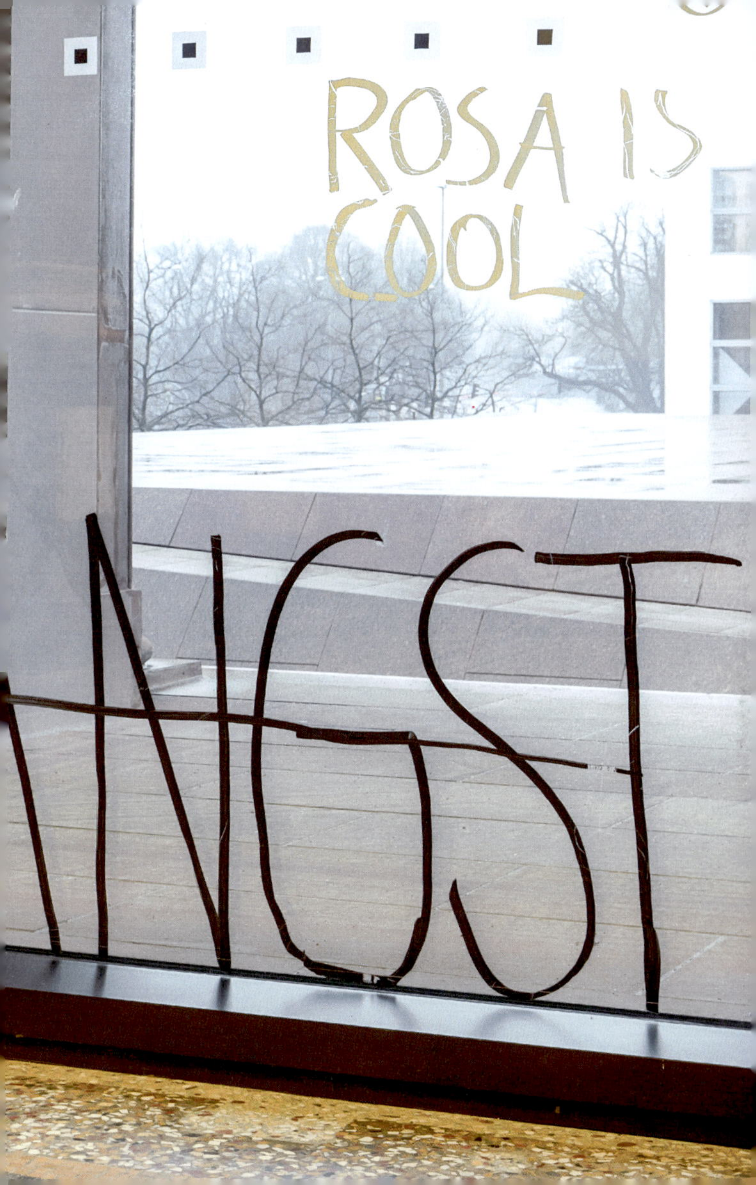

ROSA IS
COOL
NEST

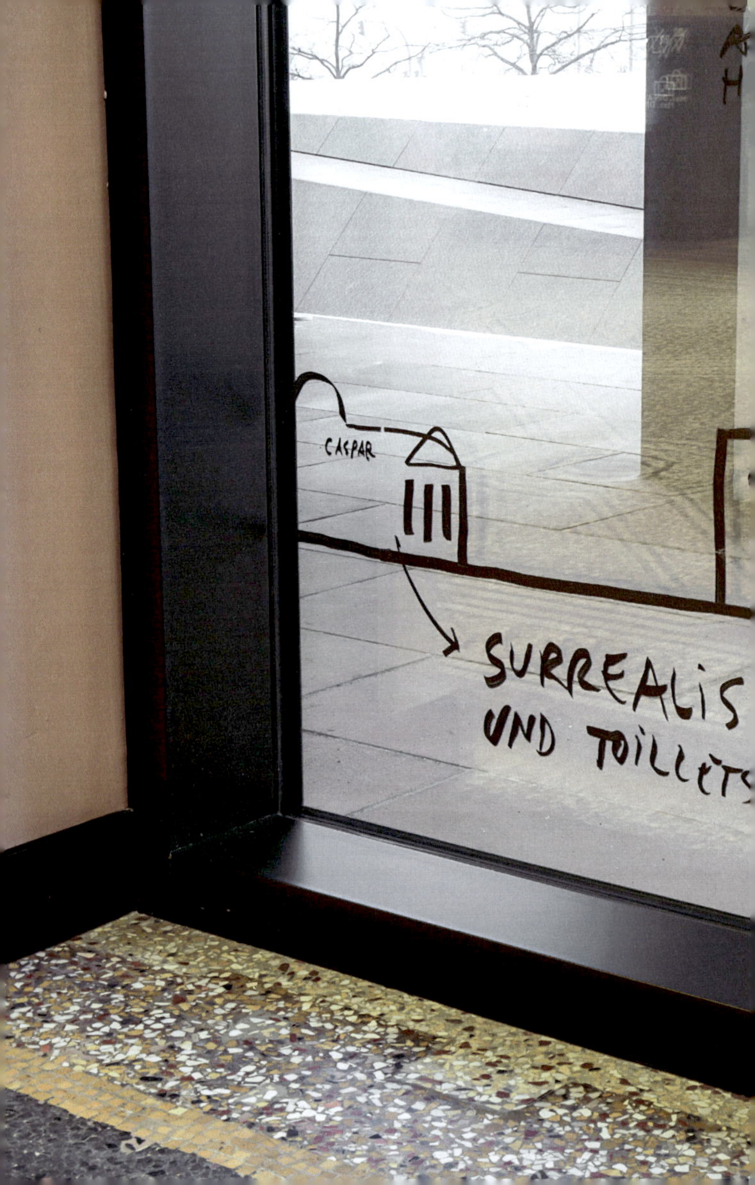

CASPAR
SURREALIS
UND TOILLETS

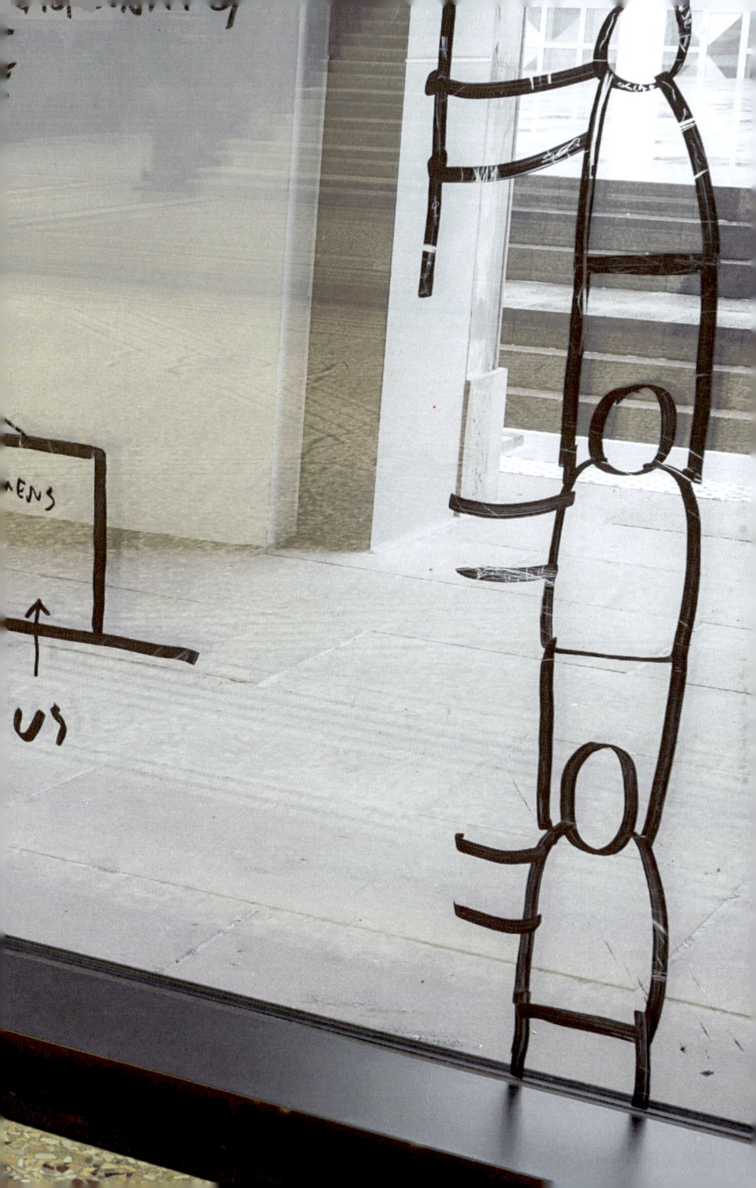
ENS
US

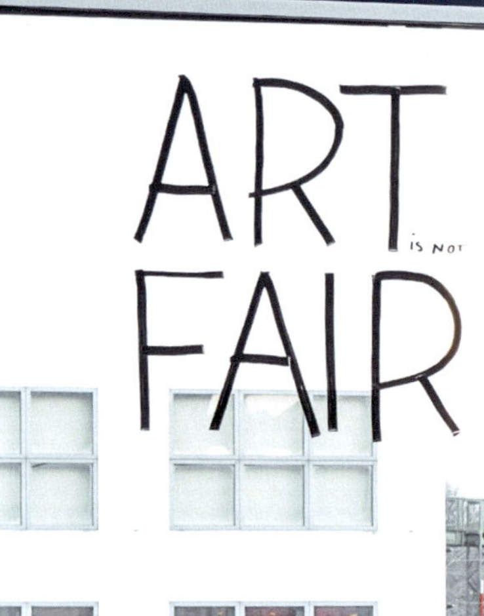

TRUMPUSSY
ART
is not
FAIR
VIRTUAL REALITY IS THE REALITY
GOT FRIENDS
THOUSANDS OF THEM

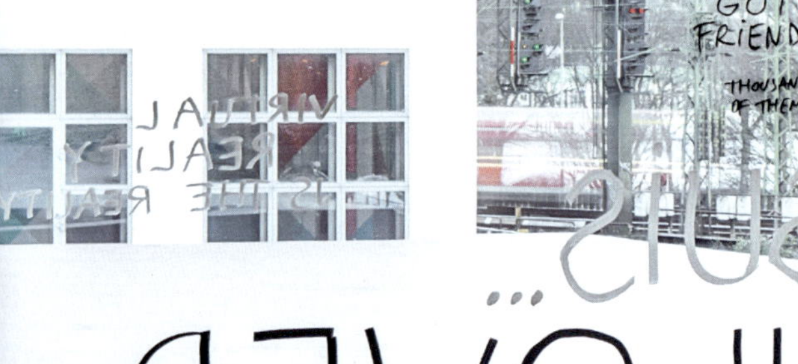

...OVER
THE OTHER SIDE IS BETTER

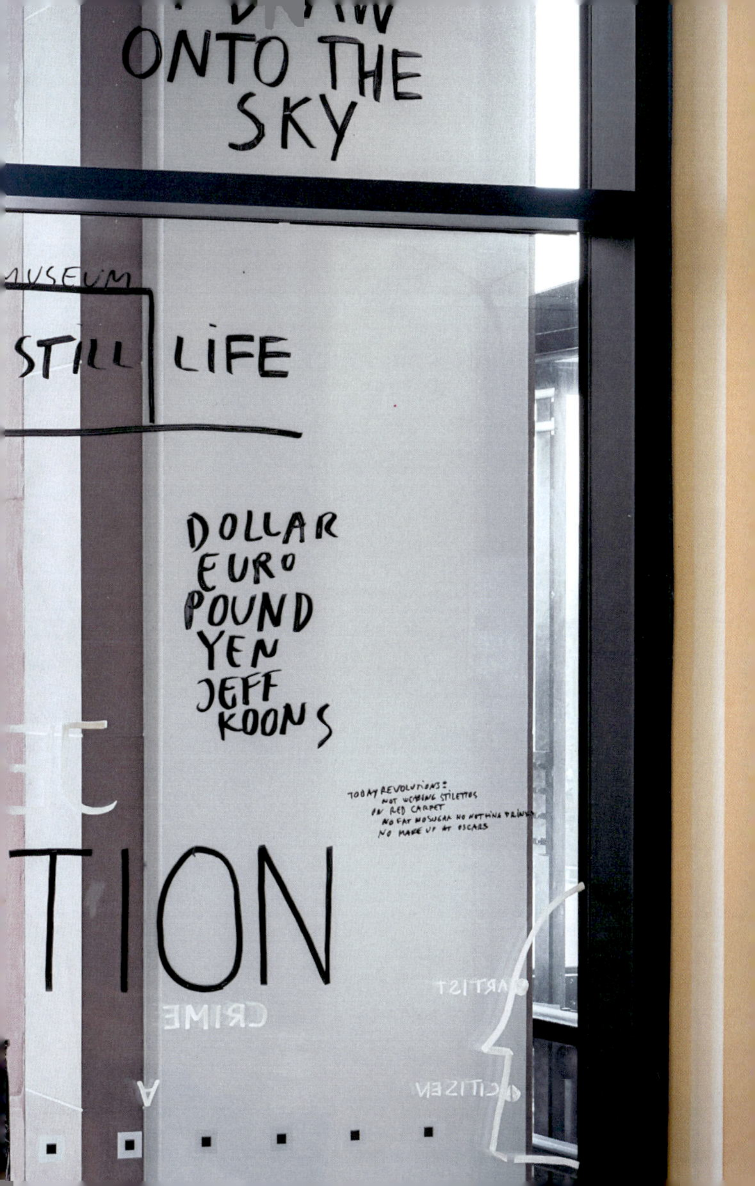

DRAW
ONTO THE
SKY

MUSEUM

STILL LIFE

DOLLAR
EURO
POUND
YEN
JEFF
KOONS

TODAY REVOLUTIONS:
NOT WEARING STILETTOS
IN RED CARPET
NO FAT NOSUGAR NO NOTHING DRINKS
NO MAKE UP AT OSCARS

TION

ARTIST

CRIME

CITIZEN

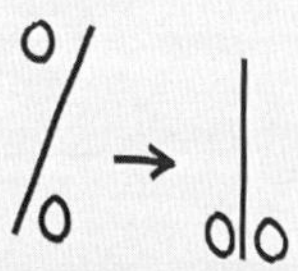

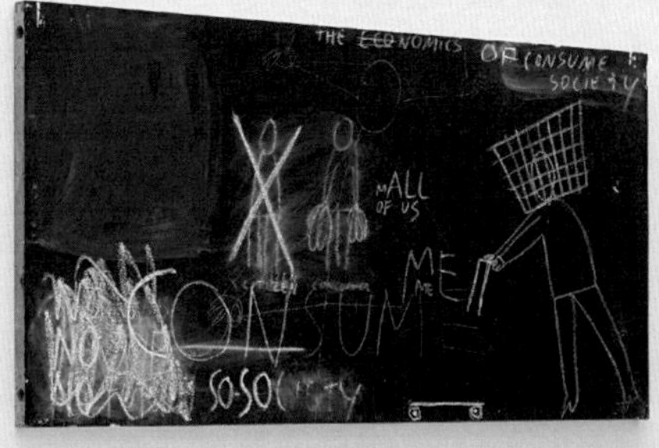

RICH NATION BROKEN JEANS

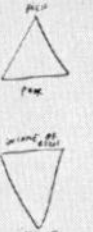

FROM BIG
BANG
TO
BIG MAC

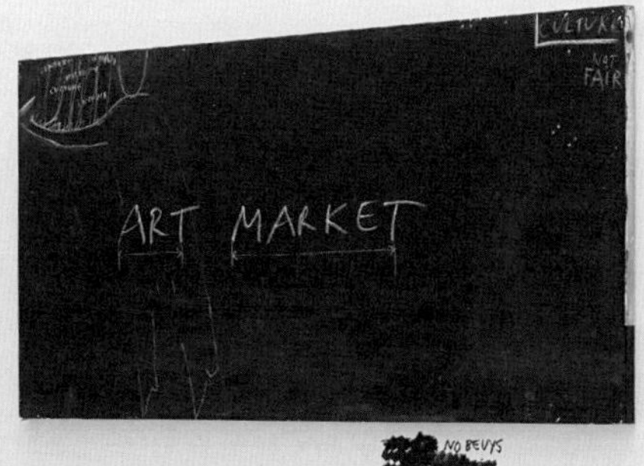
CULTURE NOT FAIR
ART MARKET
NO BEUYS
NO TEACHING
KunsTHALLE
OLD   NEW
GOT
ROSA

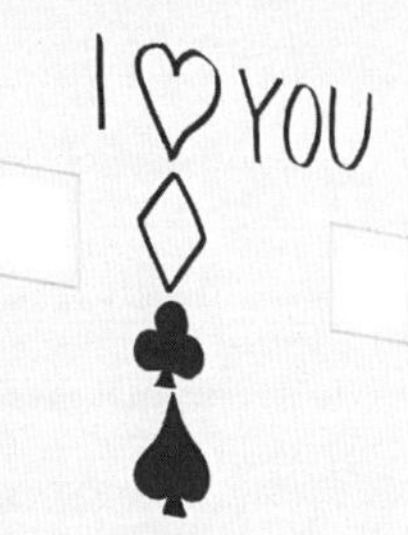

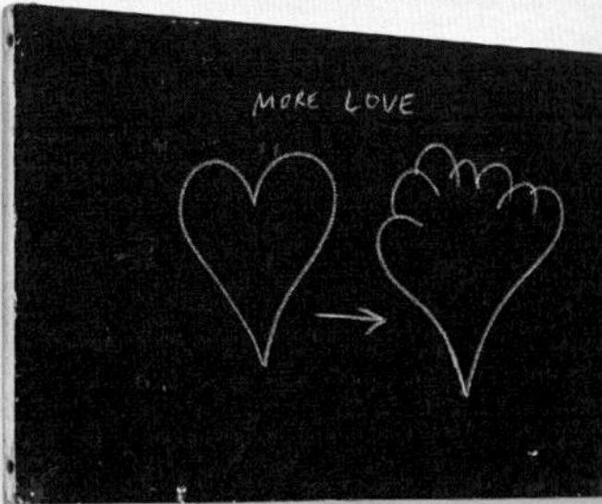

LOVE ME
BEFORE
I GET FAT

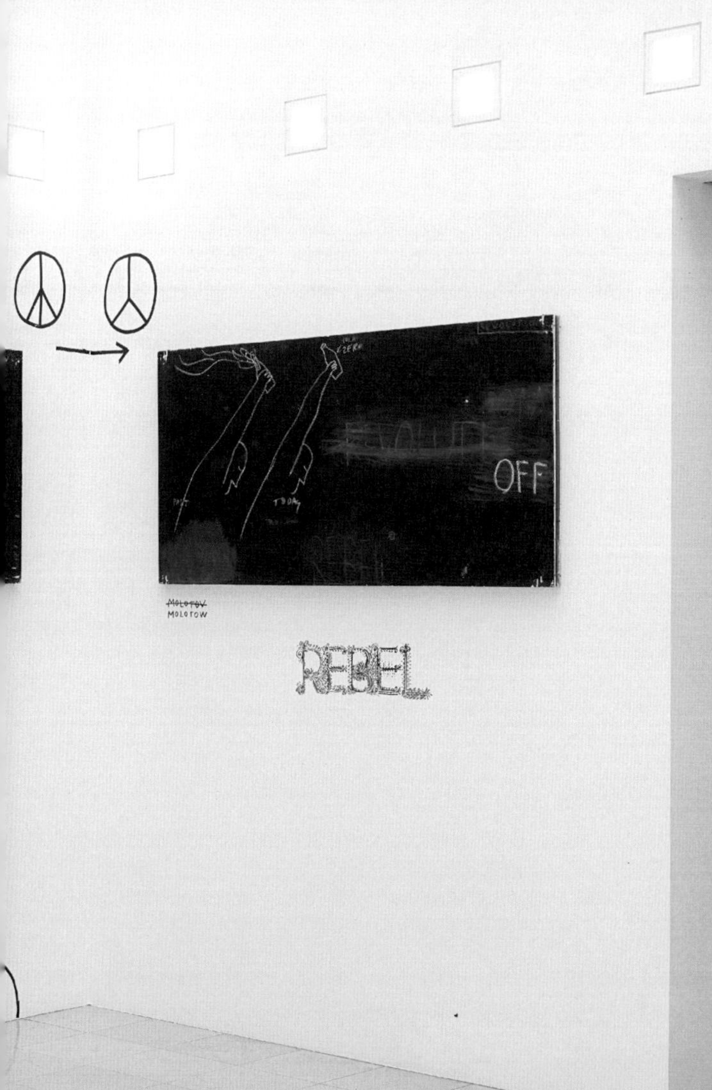
OFF
MOLOTOV
MOLOTOW
REBEL

WE ARE GETTING
CLOSE TO THE '30TIES
THE 2030

THE GREAT
FEARS:

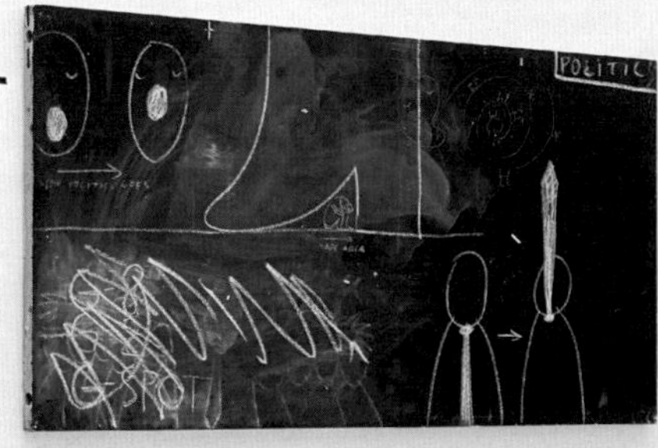

'30TIES   NOW

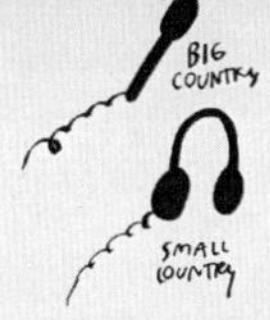

BERLIN WALL

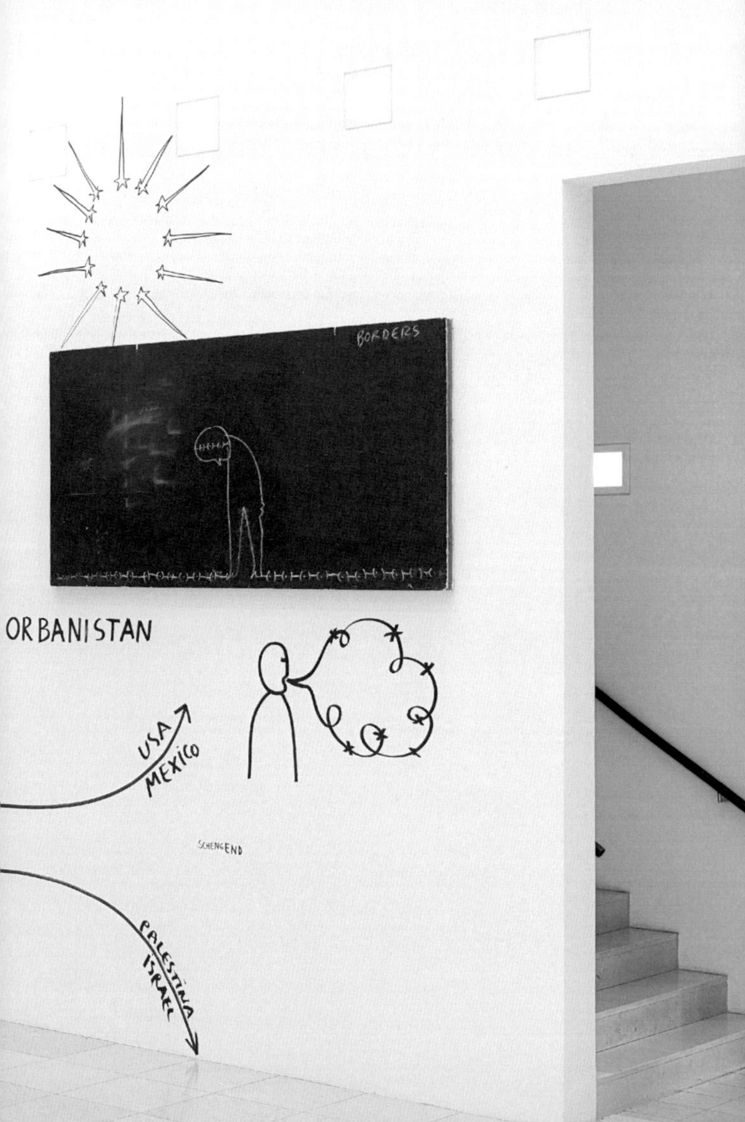

BORDERS
ORBANISTAN
USA
MEXICO
SCHENGEND
PALESTINA
ISRAEL

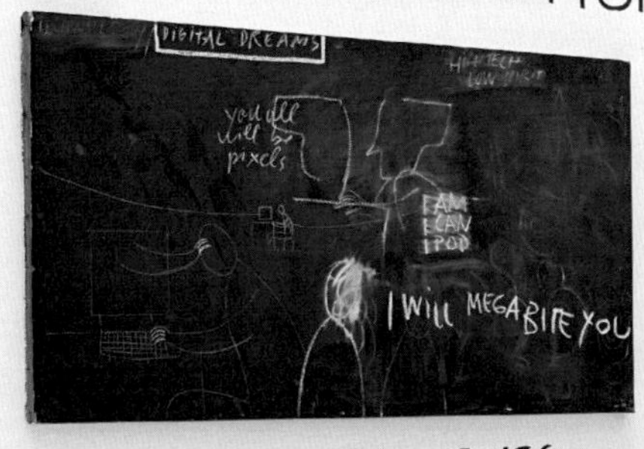

FLAT SCREEN 3D MOVIES

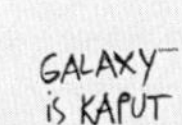

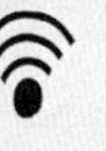

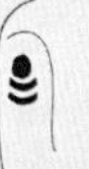

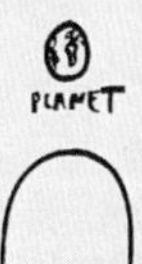

PLANET DATA

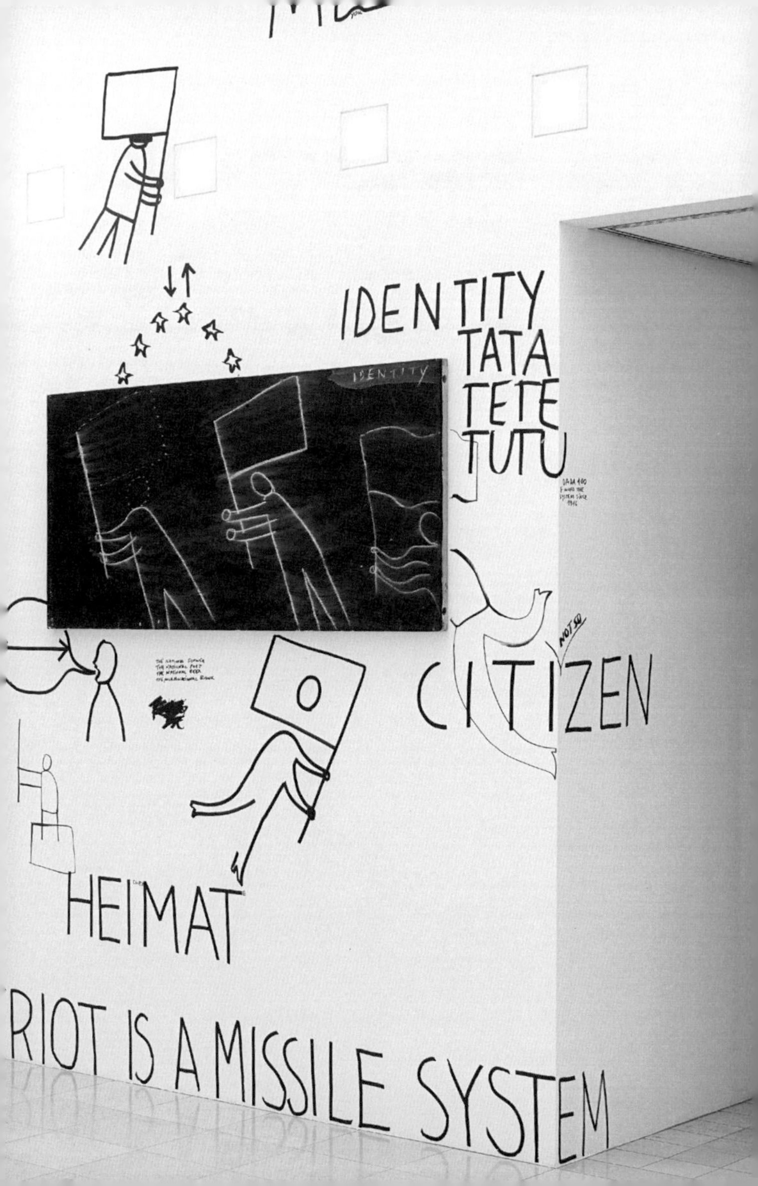

IDENTITY
TATA
TETE
TUTU

IDENTITY

CITIZEN

HEIMAT

RIOT IS A MISSILE SYSTEM

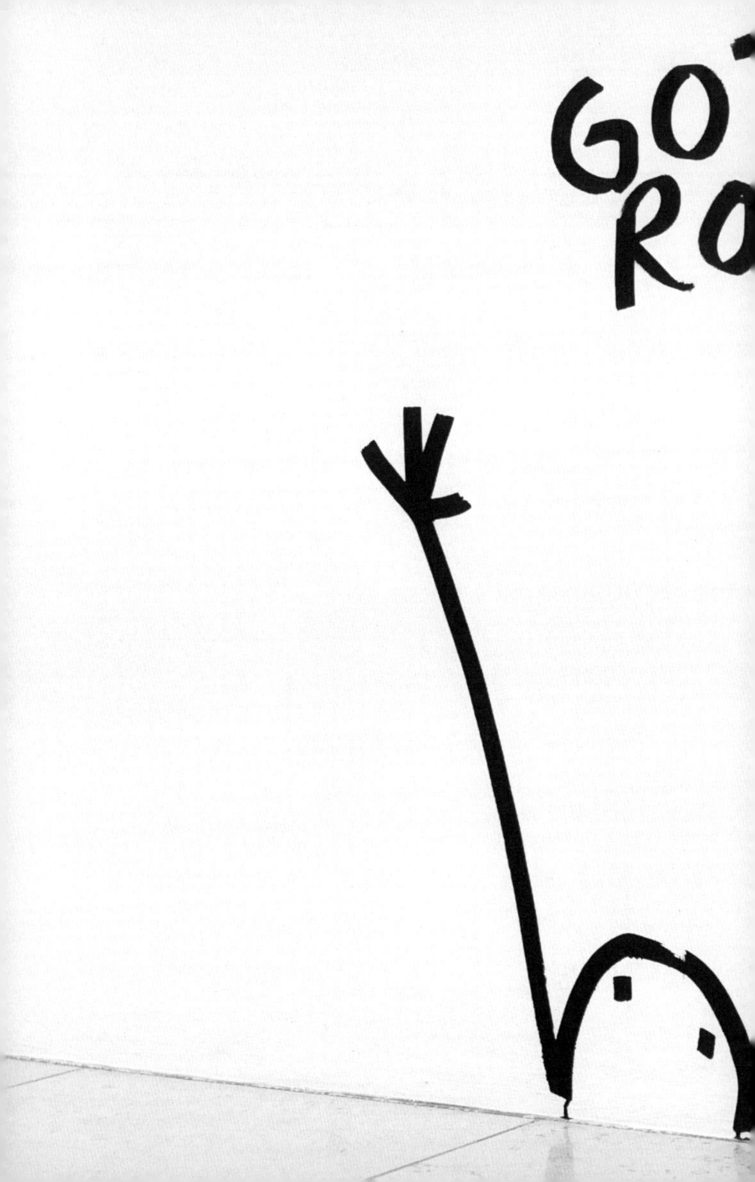
GO
RO

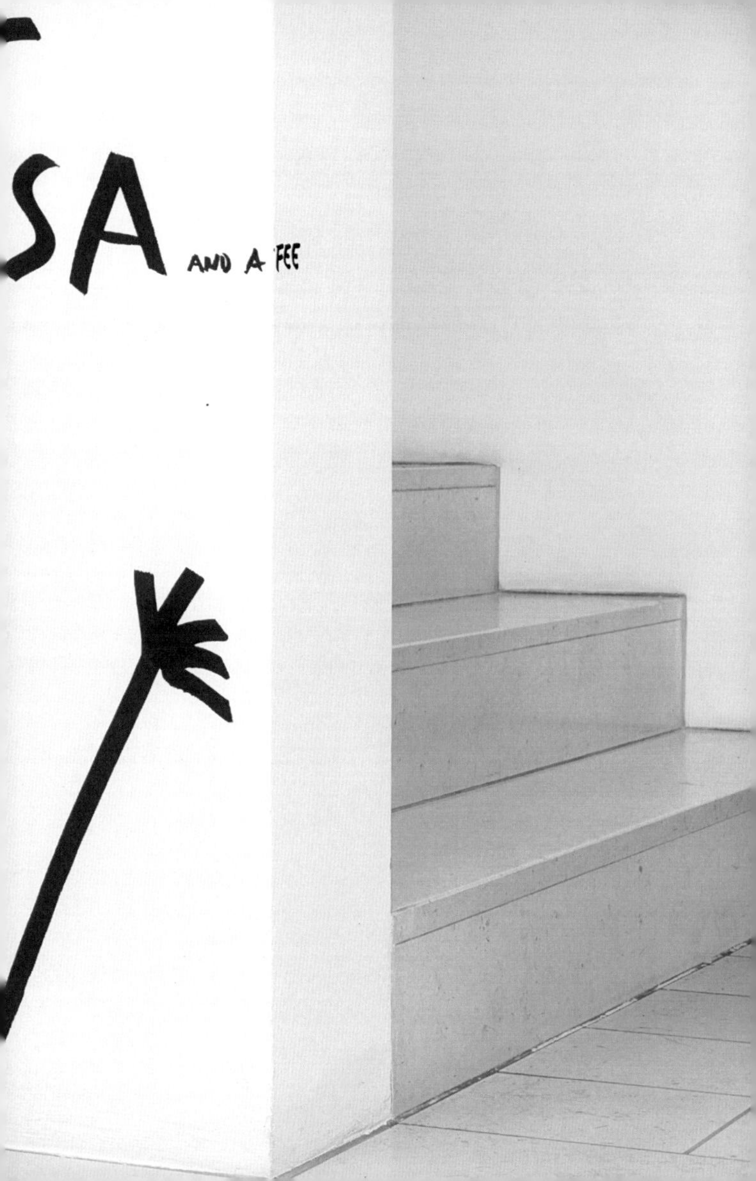
SA
AND A FEE

Impressum / Colophon

2016 erhielt Dan Perjovschi den erstmals verliehenen Rosa-Schapire-Kunstpreis der Freunde der Kunsthalle e.V.
Juror: Kasper König auf Einladung von Hubertus Gaßner, ehemaliger Direktor der Hamburger Kunsthalle
In 2016 Dan Perjovschi received the first-ever Rosa Schapire Art Prize, awarded by the friends' society of the Hamburger Kunsthalle. The juror was Kasper König, on the invitation of Hubertus Gaßner, former director of the Hamburger Kunsthalle

Diese Publikation basiert auf dem Skizzenbuch des Künstlers Dan Perjovschi, das in Vorbereitung seiner Ausstellung „Rosa Schapire Art Prize 2016: Dan Perjovschi", 15. Oktober 2016 – 29. Januar 2017 entstand. Das Skizzenbuch befindet sich heute als Geschenk des Künstlers Dan Perjovschi, seiner Galerie Gregor Podnar, Berlin, sowie der Freunde der Kunsthalle e.V. in der Sammlung der Hamburger Kunsthalle (Inv. 2016-61-1).
This publication is based on the sketchbook artist Dan Perjovschi produced in preparation for the exhibition "Rosa Schapire Art Prize 2016: Dan Perjovschi", which ran from 15 October 2016 to 29 January 2017. The sketchbook was given to the Hamburger Kunsthalle for its collection by the artist in conjunction with his gallery Gregor Podnar in Berlin and the Freunde der Kunsthalle e.V. (Inv. 2016-61-1).

Kuratoren / Curators: Brigitte Kölle, Kasper König

Hamburger Kunsthalle
Glockengießerwall 5
20095 Hamburg
Tel: +49 (0) 428131-200
Fax: +49 (0) 42854-3409
www. hamburger-kunsthalle.de

Herausgeben von / edited by: Brigitte Kölle
im Auftrag der / on behalf of Hamburger Kunsthalle

Fotografie / Photography: Christoph Irrgang
Installationsaufnahmen/ Installation shots: Kay Riechers
Druck / Print: Bookfactory GmbH, Stadthagen

Erschienen bei / First published by Koenig Books Ltd
at the Serpentine Gallery
Kensington Gardens
London W2 3XA
www.koenigbooks.co.uk

Bibliografische Information der Deutschen Nationalbibliothek. Die Deutsche
Nationalbibliothek verzeichnet diese Publikation in der Deutschen National-
bibliografie; detaillierte bibliografische Daten sind über http://dnb.d-nb.de
abrufbar.

Bibliographic information published by the Deutsche Nationalbibliothek
The Deutsche Nationalbibliothek lists this publication in the Deutsche Nati-
onalbibliografie; detailed bibliographic data are available in the Internet at
http://dnb.d-nb.de.

Printed in Germany

Vertrieb / Distribution:

**Germany, Austria, Switzerland / Europe
Buchhandlung Walther König**
Ehrenstr. 4,
D - 50672 Köln
Tel: +49 (0) 221 / 20 59 6 53
verlag@buchhandlung-walther-koenig.de

**UK & Ireland
Cornerhouse Publications Ltd. - HOME**
2 Tony Wilson Place
UK – Manchester M15 4FN
Tel: +44 (0) 161 212 3466
publications@cornerhouse.org

**Outside Europe
D.A.P. / Distributed Art Publishers, Inc.**
75 Broad Street, Suite 630
USA - New York, NY 10004
Tel: +1 (0) 212 627 1999
enadel@dapinc.com

ISBN 978-3-96098-412-2

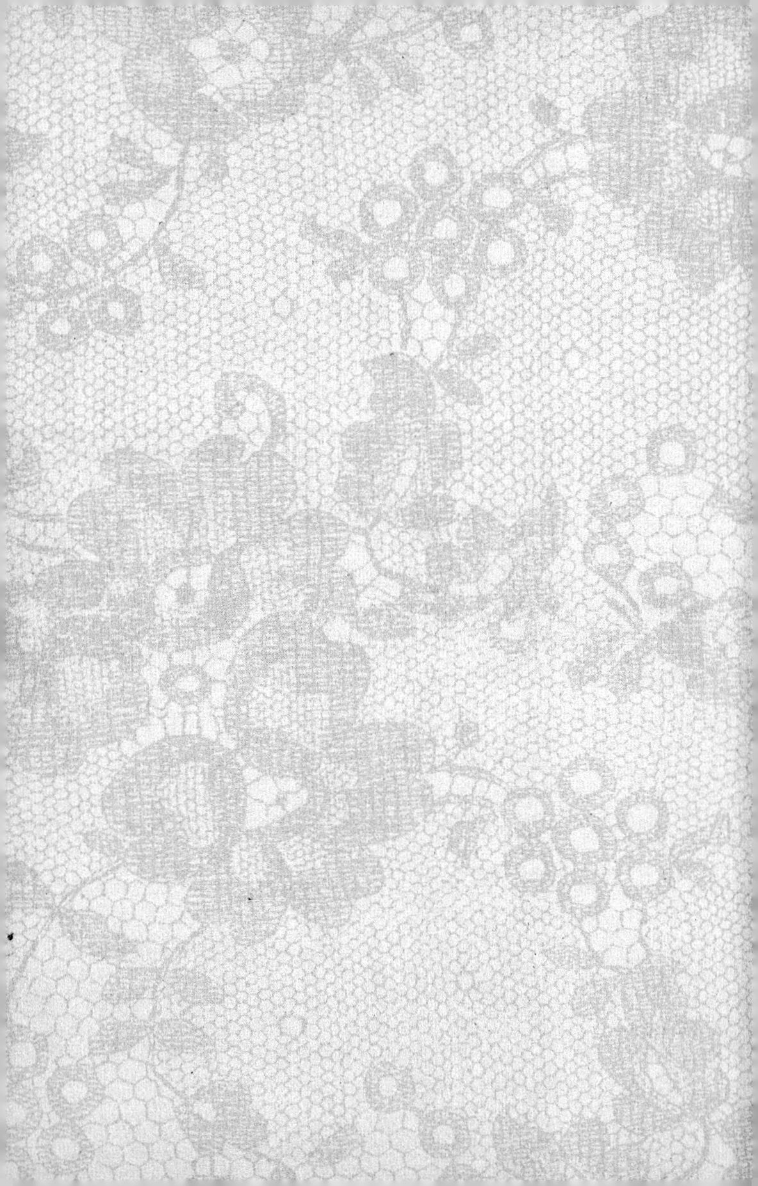